W9-BLS-644

This
Great Land

Scenic Splendors of America

This Great Land

Scenic Splendors of America

Photography by
David Muench

Rand McNally & Company
Chicago • New York • San Francisco

Book design by Mili Thompson

*The editors gratefully acknowledge the assistance
of Verne Huser in completing this project.*

Copyright © 1983 Rand McNally & Company
All rights reserved
Printed in the United States of America
First printing, 1983

Library of Congress Cataloging in Publication Data

Muench, David.
   This great land.

   1. United States—Description and travel—1981–
Views.   I. Title.
E169.04.M83 1983   917.3   83–9529
ISBN 0–528–81120–7

Overleaf– COLORADO RIVER FROM DEAD HORSE POINT, CANYONLANDS COUNTRY / UTAH

To all Americans who inherit the guardianship of this land . . .
And to David Sumner, who loved the land and worked to preserve its wildness.

D.M.

HATTERAS LIGHTHOUSE,
CAPE HATTERAS NATIONAL SEASHORE / NORTH CAROLINA

Contents

VERNAL FALLS, YOSEMITE NATIONAL PARK / CALIFORNIA

PHOTOGRAPHING AMERICA:
A Personal Voyage

THE PHOTOGRAPHS ASSEMBLED IN THIS COLLECTION ARE a celebration of the American landscape. My continuing need to give creative expression to my love for the original, pristine landscape has taken me across our country, with camera in hand, to search for the "spirit of place" in this great land.

Nowhere on this revolving orb in space is Nature more lavish with her expression than here in America. A swelling of national pride goes with a mention of the Grand Canyon, Yellowstone, Yosemite, the mighty Mississippi, or the Great Smoky Mountains.

The landscape can be at once universal and intensely personal. It can be as expansive as Nevada's distant horizons, or as intimate as an unfolding butterfly orchid in the Everglades. Such disparate phenomena as these are nurtured by the same simple ingredients—sun, water, land, and space, along with time—the basic elements that make up the natural landscape.

Contrasts within the land mass we call America are astounding. A great melting pot of people, America hints at an equally varied mix of landforms. In the West, epic geologic forces hold a 3,500-year-old sequoia against the slopes of granite peaks, while in the rain shadow a few miles distant a lone primrose blooms on a sand ripple in the Mojave Desert. Farther on lives a knarled, windswept piece of sculpture called the bristlecone pine, a dwarf beside its sequoia neighbor but even centuries older.

Advancing and retreating glaciers deposited rich loam up and down the Mississippi waterway; but when sheets of ice blanketed New England for centuries, they scoured its rocks and left it lean of soil. In the glacially spared Smoky Mountains an unusual and diversified plant community has developed through the eons, while half a continent away lie the salt-laden dry playas of the Great Basin, where a seed will not take hold.

The Continental Divide threads the spine of America through the Rocky Mountains, where earth and sky blend in a clear vision of rock wilderness, and one can envision the earth in its original state. At times it seems to me as if our planet spins from the axis of this great range.

America's natural diversity is a visible reminder of earth's ever mysterious rhythms, and these rhythms are a source of inspiration for my photographic search.

The landscape, even its bare rock, is never static; it changes constantly with the tranformation of light. What light defines by its drawing of forms, textures, and patterns needs only a discerning eye to complete the photograph. The color we see also results from light. Dawn and evening best bring out the warmer tones. Breaks between great clouds or storms are powerful for setting mood. In the absence of direct sunlight, soft, natural tones release the quiet, more intimate subtleties. An unusual sense of timing is most important for bringing the subject in harmony with the elusiveness of changing light.

Patience, too, is a necessity, whether waiting out a lightning storm at timberline in the San Francisco Peaks, or attempting to photograph the red maple autumn color changes in Maine.

Water, in all its forms, is an integral part of nature. The streams are the arteries and veins of the surface of the living earth. During springtime in the East and the southern mountains, flowing water plays a natural part in almost every picture, as waterfalls and rushing brooks and rapids. Beaches, marshes, bayous, and swamps reflect this rich season. "A lake is the landscape's most beautiful and expressive feature," said Henry David Thoreau. "It is earth's eye."

Photographically I try to integrate a foreground of rocks or plant forms into my composition. The inner structure of the Appalachians or Rockies can be realized more readily by thrusting the limestone or granite into view or by including a close rhododendron detail where the unusual delicate design is apparent. The impact of this near/far composition involves the viewer in a three-dimensional experience and, it is hoped, leads to greater appreciation of the land.

As humans pressed by the demands of various materialistic pursuits, we are drawn to the spectacle of an elemental Nature, tuning a rhythm within us to the rhythms of the land. The changes of the seasons, the cycle of passing day from sunup to sundown, the interplay of light and shadow, of rock, wood, and stream, of desert, cliff, and valley—all of these restore our sense of well-being. We seek instinctively to return to a simpler, more primitive haven to defend ourselves against cultural pressures.

The spirit of this land nurtures our spirit of freedom, freedom that must be guarded, fostered, and fought for, for its own sake and because it is the wellspring of our very existence. A commitment to hold technology in check and preserve our wild lands, to maintain a balance between economy and ecology, is vital for future generations. Let us hope that the combined effort in this volume will help to heighten our awareness of and caring for the precious American landscape we have taken so long for granted.

David Muench

All photographs in this collection were made with a 4 × 5 large-format Linhof Teknika, using primarily daylight Ektachrome film. Exposures were calculated from a Weston light meter. Focal lengths for lenses are 65mm through 1,000mm. Filtration is sparingly used, to fill a gap between what is seen and what the film actually records. A tripod is used in all cases.
D. M.

DAWN, NAUSET MARSH, CAPE COD NATIONAL SEASHORE / MASSACHUSETTS

The Northeast

A Stubborn, Enduring Corner of America

BY CASKIE STINNETT

THE POWERFUL BEAUTY OF WOODS AND shore sweeps across this vast continent, but in the Northeast it seems to have a redolence, a pastoral strength of its own, especially in that corner of America known as New England. Stormy seas pound the worn boulders of the coast of Maine, tossing spray high into the air, where it is caught by the fitful sea wind and blown across the tops of the spruce and pine. Across the rolling meadows of Vermont and New Hampshire, ancient fences of fieldstone create strange geometric patterns, and in the low areas there are great thickets of alder, birch, and goldenrod. Curtains of snow move down the rocky shore of the North Atlantic, shrouding the coastlines of Massachusetts, Rhode Island, and Connecticut, and bringing a premature darkness to a winter day. But in late April, the voice of the whippoorwill sounds in the evening air, a flutelike announcement that spring has arrived, that life endures, that the fields and the woods will become youthful again, and that the sunshine will once more warm the earth. There is an excitement, a stimulation to be found in the seasons of New England that

I think exists nowhere else in this country.

It has been said that landscapes form the character of the people they shelter, and there is a great deal to recommend this theory. Lawrence Durrell once expressed the belief that you could exterminate the French at a blow and resettle the country with Tartars, and within two generations discover, to your astonishment, that the national characteristics of the French were prevalent once again. Human beings, he was convinced, are expressions of their landscape. When I think of the New Englander, I detect traces of the original Massachusetts Bay colonist in his flinty manner, his frugality, his determination to strip away nonsense from fact, his ability to deal competently with hardship.

When Ralph Waldo Emerson dropped by the Concord jail to visit his friend Henry David Thoreau, who had refused to pay taxes of which he disapproved, he inquired, ''Why are you here?'' There was a moment's silence, and Thoreau replied: ''Why aren't you?'' I once spent a quiet afternoon talking with Rachel Carson, and she told me that at her home on the coast of Maine she would bring small samples of

Connecticut
Delaware
Maine
Maryland
Massachusetts
New Hampshire
New Jersey
New York
Pennsylvania
Rhode Island
Vermont

seawater up from the tidal pools to examine under her microscope, but, she added, she always returned the sample to the sea when she had finished with it. When I laughed and said I hardly thought the balance of nature would be upset by a spoonful of seawater, she said, ''Then you will think I'm crazy when I tell you that if those small creatures are going to survive they must be returned to the sea at the same tide level from which I took them.'' She was silent a moment. ''This means,'' she went on slowly, ''that sometimes I must set my alarm clock and put on a robe in the middle of the night and walk to the sea and put them back.''

The spirit of Thoreau and Miss Carson lingers in New England; what appears to be self-sufficiency is really a recognition of the need for mutual forbearance. The landscape of New England is rich, with its rivers, lakes, forests, mountains, and seashore, but the New Englander is frugal by nature and will not exhaust them. Large areas of the United States have been thoughtlessly laid bare, but deep in the heart of the New Englander is the belief that nature's primal capacity to renew and to continue to provide is not unlim-

ited, and that man will ultimately have to reduce his demands upon the earth.

Character moderates and softens as one moves south. New York and Pennsylvania can have cold winters, but autumn lasts longer and spring comes earlier and the cruel sting of the New England winter is lacking. If there is truly an alliance between character and climate, the Northeast states would seem to prove it. The clean church spires and village greens of the New England states persist through New York, northern New Jersey, and Pennsylvania, but are seldom seen farther south. And the stringent austerity of the early Calvinists and the Shakers, still an influence in New England, is mellowed by the German Catholics. The Amish of Pennsylvania struggle to retain the purity of the simple life in defiance of contemporary thought and fashion.

City and country too often coexist on uneasy terms. In America, as in other countries, it is the rural population that remains the force that binds human beings to the earth and to the climate. Although the states of the Northeast are heavy with industry, they all possess large rural areas that cushion

the impact of industrial assault upon the environment and preserve the sometimes precarious balance between economy and ecology.

Since the first place that the morning sun shines upon the continental United States is Mount Katahdin in Maine, that state makes a logical point from which to begin a ramble across the sometimes bucolic, often rugged, enduring Northeast. The coast of Maine is a magnificent sight, a landscape of exalted expectancy. No other land, except perhaps Norway and Finland, possesses the same character. Spruce and fir trees grow in a dark green shadow to the sea's edge; waves break against wild ledges, sending spray high into the air, where rainbows are spun for a brilliant second from spume. Bleak headlands of sheer rock quiet the winter seas, and in the silent coves and reaches blue herons stand in the water searching for minnows or some other sea creature venturing out on the low tide at twilight.

Tides control the life of coastal Maine, as the heartbeat maintains life in the body. Under spring tide conditions, they rise and fall 35 feet or more, especially where Nova Scotia curves around to the east of Maine to form the Bay of Fundy. Some of these tidal flows create a witch's broth that can be disastrous to inexperienced sailors. Great, turbulent "northeasters" bear down upon coastal Maine in winter, lashing the villages with sleet and snow, while gale winds tear at anything that is not tightly secured. On clear winter nights

the temperature plunges and the whole country seems to be lying frozen in the moonlight. But in late March or early April, cakes of ice suddenly break off and begin to move on the full, outgoing tide, docks come alive with lobstermen and fishermen, and by June the icy grip of winter is just a memory as summer visitors begin to appear.

A place of extremes, Maine is seldom the same—sometimes shadowy and obscure, sometimes splendidly sunlit. I know this land well because I live on a small island in Casco Bay for five months or more every year, and I've seen the great fluctuations in its weather, from the humid haze that enshrouds the coast in summer to the cruel cold of winter. There are the heavy fogs, which can enfold the world in a gray blanket for days on end while dismal foghorns echo endlessly across the water; and the summer storms, which roll in with jagged forks of lightning and crashing thunder, only to subside, with fury spent, in a gentle drizzle of rain through which the afternoon sun shines with a strange chartreuse glow.

A still twilight on the Maine coast is a time of beauty, especially when the tide is flowing, covering the dark secrets of the seaworld and creeping across the low stones, invading the crevices in the rocks. A few mussel shells will float on the incoming swell, but the slightest ripple in the surface will cause them to sink. A dark grotto under a rock will begin to fill, giving off a strange clapping sound, as though ap-

Overleaf–SUNRISE, CAPE COD NATIONAL SEASHORE / MASSACHUSETTS

Left– COASTLINE, CAMDEN HARBOR / MAINE

Below– STONINGTON HARBOR / MAINE

plause is coming for some unseen performance. The wind springs up, shifts quickly, and the rich, moist odor of salt marsh grass is borne on the evening air. When the moon is full, it rises in the east while the western sky is still light, laying down a path of gold in the sea. That is a breathtaking sight, made all the more overwhelming by the silence that has seized the stage. There is only the sound of the incoming tide slapping gently on the rocks as the immense copper ball turns slowly to burnished gold and rises in the sky. In the shallows a clump of rockweed bobs gently, and from somewhere far away comes a blue heron's complaint, hoarse and solemn and sad. Here on these rocks there is something marvelously infectious, something sensual and profound. So much of the coast of Maine is as it always has been.

From Kittery, in southern Maine, to Calais, where the state first touches New Brunswick, Canada, the coastline is less than 250 miles for an airborne creature, but the coves, reaches, bays, and inlets provide the state with 3,478 miles of waterfront—one-half of the tidal line of the entire eastern littoral of the United States.

Inland, the Maine countryside changes abruptly. Gone are the coastal plains; first the country is rolling and then it becomes rough, even primitive. The landscape is dominated by wilderness and lakes, with deep forests and bogs. Here the dark recesses of woodland are difficult to reach, at times inaccessible except by foot; and although the hunting and fishing are unrivaled, the black flies and mosquitoes of summer can be brutal, and only the most dedicated sportsmen can withstand their attack for long. Wildlife abounds. Moose are now so plentiful in this country that in the fall of 1982 the state reopened a long-closed moose hunting season. The north woods is one of the few places in the nation where landlocked salmon still can be found.

The first escarpments of the massive Appalachian Mountain range rise in western Maine, New Hampshire, Vermont, and New York. The Appalachians are to the East what the

Rockies are to the West. They constitute a nearly continuous chain of mountains stretching all the way to Alabama, running roughly parallel to the Atlantic Seaboard. First formed by catastrophic upheavals in the earth's crust, then molded by eroding action of glaciers and rivers, the Appalachians are among the oldest mountains on earth.

Although the Appalachians pervade the Northeast and provide rural areas and even remote wilderness, there also exists in this corner of the nation that anomaly known as the Megalopolis. The pattern of human settlement that it entails cannot be ignored. Historically, the density of settlement in America has depended upon the agricultural capacity of the land to support its population, although the length of time a region has been settled also plays an important part. How, then, did the Northeast become the country's first great center of commerce and urban sprawl? Why has the seaboard region extending from Portland, Maine, to Washington, D.C., grown to be the third greatest population center in the world,

with about 45 million people? If it cannot be explained in terms of physical terrain, of landscapes, of convenient rivers and harbors, and temperate climate, perhaps one has to fall back upon the historical concept that this was the first landfall of the major European colonists, the first center of urbanization. From here the country grew to the south and the west as threats from unfriendly Indians and other external dangers diminished. Whatever explains the Megalopolis theory, one thing is certain. The rural areas of the Northeast are hospitable to this high density population; extensive agricultural areas serve the needs of the region's urban dwellers, with fresh vegetables, fruit, and milk, and the forested areas of the central and northern Appalachians satisfy many of their recreational needs.

Vermont and most of New Hampshire are largely divorced from the dense urban concentration found closer to the Atlantic Coast. Here the land sweeps westward toward Lake Ontario in a series of neat meadows, rolling hills, and

Left– VIEW OF LITTLE RIVER VALLEY, FROM MOUNT MANSFIELD / VERMONT

Above– QUARTZ LEDGE IN GREAT GULF WILDERNESS, PRESIDENTIAL RANGE / NEW HAMPSHIRE

the taller peaks of Vermont's Green Mountain range. The mountains are accurately named; there is a greenness here—even in the lowlands—that one seldom encounters. The meadows stretch across the landscape and enclose the brooks and streams and hedgerows. In the late afternoon, a pale sky fades above the misty trees of the low meadows, the willows and birch and beech, and only in densely forested mountain ranges are there the hazy green and blue and purple for which the region is famous. In the winter, snow drifts across the farther mountains, now hiding, now revealing those forests of spruce and pine that grow so densely in the Green Mountains. Basically, this is rural country with few cities, and because it is a rugged, inland area its people are inclined—indeed forced—to be self-reliant and individualistic. This does not mean that they are antisocial; rather their rural outposts become the sanctuary for their own way of life, which differs markedly from that of the industrial and coastal towns.

On countless hillsides between the sea and the Adirondack Mountains, and even on the low ranges of the Green Mountains, are America's great maple forests, which glow in autumn like a forest fire, and produce what many consider the most spectacularly blinding foliage in the entire nation. These forests also produce a large part of the country's maple syrup. Sugaring was a lesson the early settlers of this region learned from the Indians, who had long known how to boil the sap of the maple and convert it into sugar and syrup.

The Indians induced the flow of sap by cutting a V-shaped slash in the bark, letting it flow into a wooden trough. The white settler modified the technique by inserting a spout in the tree and catching the sap in a wooden bucket. Today, this improvement has generally been discarded in favor of plastic tubing, which carries the sap all the way to the modern collecting tank.

In the deep valley between the Green Mountains and the Adirondacks, where the land drops off to form Lake Champlain and Lake George, is some of America's most majestic country. I first saw Lake George many years ago and was stunned by the beauty of its blue surface reflecting the sunlight of a bright October morning, while to the west of me on a hillside the forest blazed in its autumn coat. South of Lake George, the Hudson River Valley commences, threaded by the Hudson River, which flows from Lake Tear of the Clouds in the Adirondacks all the way to the Atlantic Ocean at New York Bay. The Hudson's channel is said to extend more than 100 miles into the ocean to the end of the continental shelf.

New York's beautiful and fertile river valleys form a gigantic geographical Y, the Hudson being the right arm and the Mohawk River the left. With the opening of the Erie Canal in 1825, the Hudson River was linked to the Great Lakes, and eastern New York had, for the first time, a water route to the west. The Hudson River Valley and, to some

Left– FIRST SNOW, MOUNT GREYLOCK / MASSACHUSETTS

Below– LAKES OF THE CLOUDS AND RIDGES FROM TOP OF MOUNT WASHINGTON / NEW HAMPSHIRE

extent, the Mohawk Valley are now inhabited by ghosts of an earlier and grander era, their great mansions taken over by preservation groups, their ancient canals silted up, their small river towns slumbering and forgotten. But in the Hudson Valley lie some of America's oldest vineyards, which still produce many New York State wines. Like the Rhine, whose mountainous banks are dotted with castles, and the Loire, which flows through the region of France's great chateaux, the Hudson attracted some of America's greatest fortunes, and the mansions that were built on its scenic bluffs are still among the grandest in the country.

New York's most famous vineyards are in the Finger Lakes region, on the slopes between Lake Canandaigua and Lake Keuka, where the country—now clear of the mountains—sweeps spaciously toward that strange 36-mile-wide isthmus that is divided by the Niagara River. Here a freakish drop in the river of 326 feet, most of it in a single, roaring plunge, creates Niagara Falls, still considered one of the wonders of the world.

Of the three falls that make up Niagara Falls, the American Falls and Horseshoe (Canadian) Falls are perhaps the most scenic, but many insist that Bridal Veil Falls is the most spectacular. Although the heyday of Niagara Falls was a half-century ago, there is magnetism in the cascade's grandeur yet. One of the nation's greatest scenic attractions before the days of widespread international air travel, and the honeymoon destination of countless newlyweds, the falls do not seem to have suffered from the pallor and torpidity that often result when popularity wanes. Visitors still board *The Maid of the Mist*, a sightseeing boat, and sail within yards of the roaring falls, gazing upward at the awesome sight of tons of water hurtling through the air.

In the St. Lawrence River, which sweeps from Lake Ontario to the Gulf of St. Lawrence and the Atlantic Ocean, forming what is in effect another coastal area for New York State, lie the Thousand Islands. The islands actually number more than 1,700; some are hardly larger than an exposed rock ledge while others contain homes and some even accommodate small villages. In the summer the islands seem to come alive, and the residents have the superb river for their playground. The channels and small inlets are at their door. For miles, motorboats, sailing vessels, sleek cruisers, tankers, and freighters cruise up and down the waterway, twisting around islands and promontories, looping around buoys and channel markers, and sending small waves against the docks. Dozens of little launches ferry islanders to the mainland to do their marketing, visit the post office, or do other household errands. But in winter the great river turns silent, and the islands are seldom free of snow. Then a deeply rooted cold sweeps in from Canada, numbing everything it touches, turning the islands into abandoned outcroppings in the frozen landscape.

Still largely untouched by the spreading Megalopolis are the Berkshires in Massachusetts, the salt smell of the wharves at Gloucester and Marblehead, the ancient sea captains' mansions of Newburyport, the paradox of shifting sand dunes, cranberry bogs, and rich meadowland known as Cape Cod, the gently rolling sea islands of Nantucket and Marthas Vine-

yard, and the gentle charm of the old villages of Cape Ann. Cape Cod, that gaunt and twisted arm of the Massachusetts coastline that reaches northward before curving in again upon itself, still possesses long, isolated beaches bordered by bayberry and beach plum. In the spring, before the great throngs of tourists arrive at the Cape, and in the fall, after they leave, the villages shed the veneer of tourism, the sand dunes are largely deserted except for an occasional wanderer, clouds drop low over the horizon, and there is a stark wildness to the oceanfront. The Outer Cape is the most remote part of the area, and here one finds the Cape Cod National Seashore, set up by the National Park Service in 1961 to protect more than 44,000 acres of beaches and sand dunes.

About 10 miles offshore from Point Judith, Rhode Island, lies Block Island, a tiny sea island of high bluffs and moors. Its gentle hills and stone-walled pastures, its freshwater ponds, and its simple homes give Block Island an English atmosphere; more than anything it resembles one of the Channel Islands. The houses sparkle white in the summer sunlight, and the harsh Atlantic scours the island's beaches. In the village where the ferries dock there are a handful of small hotels, boarding houses, and restaurants, which rely mostly on the visitors who come over from Point Judith during the brief summer season. Throughout the major part of the year, Block Island remains a quiet and peaceful place, seemingly as detached emotionally from the mainland as it is physically.

Where the flat countryside of Massachusetts becomes the rolling hills of Connecticut, there is a serene landscape of small lakes, tiny patches of woodland, tobacco fields, and brooks meandering through meadows enclosed by stone fences. Upland game is plentiful in the forested hills around Litchfield, where fine cover is available, and ruffed grouse, partridge, and woodcock are common. Partridge and woodcock like the alder thickets, creek bottoms, and damp wooded areas where earthworms are plentiful, but grouse cling to high ground. There is a mellowness to the land, as opposed to the stony and defiant country farther north. One can stand on a hillside here, away from the ceaseless traffic thundering down the throughways, and see what a beautiful country this is, an enormous garden sloping gently down to Long Island Sound. Here the forests in the evening, gray with ground mist, stand out starkly against the sky; the stone fences, crumbling and picturesque, wind across the landscape dividing land for purposes long since forgotten; gloomy poplars stand sentinel beside the brooks; and a church spire rises on the horizon, a solitary reminder of the pervasive New England conscience. There is nobility here in the very air, a benignly autocratic feeling that makes one understand the passion for freedom that nourished the American Revolution and turned these fields into the battleground that they became.

The closer one gets to New York City, the more one is sucked into the vortex of the Megalopolis. But beyond the suburban cities, beyond the John Cheever country of swimming pools and tennis courts, beyond the reaches of the Merritt Parkway and the tollgates and shopping malls, beyond the coach houses and barns converted into expensive

Top– MOHAWK RIVER AT SCHENECTADY / NEW YORK

Bottom– SALT MARSH, POINT JUDITH BAY/ RHODE ISLAND

restaurants, lies rural Connecticut, and this is a different place. Here the wind blows off the sea, the rivers thread their way from the high ridges in the west through the rocks and valleys of a peaceful countryside, and the very texture of life changes. A combination of individualism and duty takes possession of the soul here, where an eccentric is more likely to be tolerated than feared, where discontent is as freely aired as agreement.

To the south a new region opens up, a region embracing the flatlands and marshes of New Jersey and Delaware, the Chesapeake Bay country of Maryland, and the mountains and plains and coalfields of Pennsylvania. Here the culture is more casual, more easygoing than that to the north. The hardships suffered by the Massachusetts Bay colonists seem to have settled into the lifestyle and personality of the New Englander, but their effect is not noticeable south of the Hudson. Instead, the people here seem to reflect more the spirit of Virginia's Jamestown Colony, where the settlers grew tobacco—hardly an essential crop—and many intermarried with Indian women. One seldom encounters the extremes of climate here, or the isolated farmhouses, the wilderness areas, the ice-gray skies of winter, or the great woodlands of the north, although there are vast forests in Pennsylvania, especially in the Pocono Mountain range.

In that great expanse of country that reaches westward across the Appalachian and Allegheny Mountains there is something for everyone. Everyone but beach lovers; this is landlocked country. It is a world of mostly unspoiled countryside. In the east along the Delaware River there are small

Left– NIAGARA FALLS / NEW YORK

Above– BUTTERMILK FALLS STATE PARK / NEW YORK

but prosperous towns scattered throughout a predominantly agricultural area, with barns decorated with hex emblems, streams running with trout, and fields of corn and wheat. Farther west are the coalfields that fire the great steel mills, where the towns are scruffier, the barns rotting, the earth more hostile; a fragmented sense of country prevails.

The Pocono Mountains, in eastern Pennsylvania, offer some of the state's most stunning scenery. To take advantage of its most pleasing prospects one should wander about in the area of Canadensis, Mount Pocono, Bushkill, and Stroudsburg. Although there are no truly magnificent, lofty peaks, as there are in the high Alleghenies, there are some rugged ranges, eventually dipping down to the Delaware Valley. There are places in Pennsylvania where the country is totally flat, totally empty, yet astonishingly beautiful. Above all else, this is a green country; nearly 2 million acres of Pennsylvania lie in protected state forests. The Susquehannock Trail System winds through 85 miles of unspoiled forest, over 2,500-foot-high mountains, across meadows strewn with wild flowers, and along rushing mountain streams.

Along Pennsylvania's eastern boundary, where the Delaware River breaks through the foothills of the Poconos at the narrow cleft known as the Delaware Water Gap, is a wooded land that reveals itself only to those who search it out. But if you travel past the motels and small inns that dot the river road and climb into the small mountains above the Delaware River, you will be rewarded by an incredible sight as the river, now broad and slow-moving, pushes its way through the last barrier before reaching the great plain that slopes to the Atlantic Ocean.

The great beaches and sand barriers all lie to the east of this country, beginning at the mouth of the harbor of New York and continuing southward as far as the Virginia capes, broken only by the natural indentations of Delaware Bay and Chesapeake Bay. Beachfronts shift, sandbars disappear, hurricanes alter dunelands, but the New Jersey, Delaware, and Maryland shorelines remain remarkably stable. Just inland from the broad sand beaches of New Jersey are the famous Pine Barrens, a desolate area of stunted and tangled pine growth, where few people live and where forgotten ghost towns were long ago swallowed up by the pine forests. Highways from Philadelphia and Trenton skirt the barrens, but no roads penetrate the isolated, still depths of this forest region. It is a lost land, and one that seems to offer no reward to a discoverer.

The large peninsula jutting into the Atlantic Ocean, bordered by Delaware Bay on the east and Chesapeake Bay on the west, is divided by Virginia, Delaware, and Maryland, with Maryland getting the lion's share. A low, ridgeless area, it is extremely hot in summer and uncomfortably cold in winter, but the soil is rich and it is a prosperous vegetable and poultry center. At Assateague Island, a barrier land in the Atlantic Ocean just off the coast of Maryland and Virginia, the Assateague Island National Seashore has been created to preserve the fragile dunes and primitive nature of this Atlantic spit. The Chesapeake Bay landscape is rural, tranquil, clean, flat. There is a tameness in the shoreline not found on the ocean coast, with small creeks emptying and filling with the tide, and the smell of fish in the air.

The sea dominates the Chesapeake Bay country, and seafood is its primary staple. Crabs, fish, and oysters crowd out all other dishes on restaurant menus. Nowhere in the world do oysters thrive so extensively as on the East Coast of the United States and the Chesapeake Bay. The Chesapeake oyster beds are among the finest, with the Chincoteagues, Lynnhavens, and smaller Rappahannocks among those favored most.

Spring comes explosively in this country. The geese go north in great droves, the ice breaks up in the freshwater ponds, and suddenly the fruit trees in the tiny orchards turn white with blossoms. Cold, rainy weather frequently comes with the end of winter, rain clouds drift in from the Atlantic Ocean, and mist and thin fog blanket the cheerless coast of the Bay. Then one day the showers end, the early summer sun appears, and a new season arrives. The woods are filled with bloodroot and May apples, skunk cabbage grows profusely in the low places, and in meadowland violets appear.

Away from the lowlands of the Chesapeake Bay, the country is flat, but soon small ridges begin to appear and behind them loom the foothills of the Blue Ridge Mountains. To the north, the meadows and small forests of Maryland climb into the Tuscarora Range and eventually into the high Alleghenies of Pennsylvania's anthracite country. There is a wild grandeur to this area, contrasting to the great plains of the upland region to the east, the latter as spectacular in its way as the former, with green fields and pasture land running away to the horizon.

This is the Northeastern corner of America, a stubborn, enduring land, where the continent rises out of the stormy North Atlantic and spreads south and west in majestic mountain ranges, green valleys, and plains. It possesses the priceless gift of variety, which it bestows extravagantly. The landscape offers the sea and rivers, great sand dunes and forests and lowlands. Four distinct seasons offer nearly every kind of weather a temperate land can provide. While the winter sea crashes upon the coast of Maine with the roar of thunder, darkness comes quietly a few hundred miles to the west, the only sound shattering the silence the voice of one loon calling to another over a waste of water. Fog may lie thick on the ocean's coast and across marshland, but elsewhere the sun shines brightly, and somewhere else it will rain; in winter snow will blanket the whole area. There is always something different to observe, to feel, to sense.

One night I heard a freight train laboring across the high Kennebec River bridge in Maine, its engine thumping and its whistle echoing mournfully in the night air. The sound would have been more mournful in other places perhaps, because it would be mourning the passage of things that were gone: the lost space, the simple life, the innocence of people turned materialistic, the great trails in the deep woods. But the mountains and the forests and the coast of the Northeast have not been spoiled. The nation began here, our government was invented here, and if landscapes can be reconciled to events, there is reason to believe that this glorious land was required for the events that transpired here.

BALD CYPRESS, TRUSSUM POND / DELAWARE

Left– ALLEGHENY RIVER FROM TIDIOUTE OVERLOOK / PENNSYLVANIA

Above– HEART LAKE, ADIRONDACK MOUNTAINS / NEW YORK

Top– TOQUE POND AND MOUNT KATAHDIN / MAINE

Bottom– WEST CORNWALL BRIDGE, HOUSATONIC RIVER / CONNECTICUT

Right– MOSS GLEN FALLS, GREEN MOUNTAINS / VERMONT

FARM ROAD THROUGH FLATLANDS, ALLEGHENY MOUNTAIN COUNTRY / PENNSYLVANIA

Left– BASS HARBOR HEAD, ACADIA NATIONAL PARK / MAINE

Above– BRENTON POINT, NEAR NEWPORT / RHODE ISLAND

Left– AUTUMN REFLECTIONS, CATOCTIN MOUNTAIN PARK / MARYLAND

Top– METAMORPHIC ROCK AND HARDWOOD FOREST, CONNECTICUT RIVER VALLEY / CONNECTICUT

Bottom– AUTUMN ALONG MULLICA RIVER, PINE BARRENS / NEW JERSEY

TIDELAND CHANNEL AND PINE HAMMOCK, CHINCOTEAGUE NATIONAL WILDLIFE REFUGE / VIRGINIA

The South

The Land Is Its Own Reward

BY CALEB PIRTLE III

THE SOUTH FOUND ISOLATION IN THE LENGTH and the breadth of its land: It has surrounded me down among the dunes of the Eastern Seaboard, and I have felt it reach back as a lonely spirit into remote, timbered pockets of Appalachian high country, finally tramping across the empty flatlands to hover like an autumn mist above the Mississippi River Valley. A wistful silence covers the landscape, broken only by the dull voice of the sea, a wind that plays its ruffles and flourishes among the magnolias, the far-off wail of a tugboat that pushes cotton from the fields to the factories. For me, the South is music, out of tune perhaps, but never out of time. The terrain is as tough as the granite in its rogue mountains, as fragile as a Piedmont wild flower that fights its way up from the mold and the mildew of the good earth. In the South I can stand alone and not be harassed by the multitudes. It is a land that tempted early settlers, then blanketed them with isolation. The land gave to them the only security they would ever have, which sometimes wasn't a lot, but it fed them and clothed them and even made a few of them prosperous.

The restless sands of the South's coastline beckoned. Mountains rose up in defiance, rewarding only those who were strong enough and stubborn enough to venture into the highlands that became home. Forests brought shade and shelter to a fruitful earth where harvests of cotton and tobacco, indigo and rice, peanuts and corn whiskey eventually broke some men and anointed others with aristocracy. Rivers became highways, quenching the thirst of the crops and giving life to settlements that begat new cities, which rose up like grand sculptures of steel and glass and chrome. Yet the soul of the South would forever lie buried deep among the roots and the riches of the land.

The Atlantic touches the beaches and the isles of the Eastern Seaboard, weaving together the heritage and the colonial traditions of Virginia, the Carolinas, Georgia, and Florida. The Gulf of Mexico sweeps gently onto the western coast of Florida, scattering spun-sugar white sands along the Miracle Strip, and its waters wash ashore among the sea oats and driftwood of Alabama and Mississippi, moving into the shifting marshes of Louisiana.

Alabama
Arkansas
Florida
Georgia
Kentucky
Louisiana
Mississippi
North Carolina
South Carolina
Tennessee
Virginia
West Virginia

Appalachia is the broad spine that links the Southern highlands. The Great Smoky Mountains keep North Carolina and Tennessee shoulder to shoulder. The Alleghenies and the Blue Ridge weld West Virginia, Virginia, and North Carolina inland from the Eastern Shore. Kentucky drops out of the Cumberland Mountains and basks in bluegrass. And Arkansas is crowned by the Ozarks' rugged peaks.

The South was settled, even tamed, by plows that broke new ground and sometimes spoiled it. In time, it belonged to the plantation lord, the farmer, the sharecropper. They fought to take the land, then fought to hold it. Wars left bloodstains upon the soil and a mournful legacy of unmarked graves strewn upon the hillsides. But the land and its promises, the Southerner has always believed, were worth the gambles and the calluses and the costs.

The Tidewater of Virginia reaches for the sea, sprawling across a low, swampy marshland that wades out among the splintered peninsulas toward the curve of Chesapeake Bay. On an April morning in 1607, the *Susan Constant*, the *Godspeed*, and the *Discovery* anchored off the Eastern Shore, and England landed its first colonists upon a narrow, vine-entangled cove that would be known as Jamestown. The colony would struggle, then prosper, then eventually decline. But the cultivation of tobacco as a money crop survived. Homesteads gradually spread out along the York, James, and Rappahannock rivers, built by men whose descendants would demand and die for independence, shouting for liberty at Williamsburg and winning it on the battlefield of Yorktown.

Throughout the Tidewater region, plantations nestle beneath the aging oaks. Thoroughbreds run the meadows. And just offshore, protected and undisturbed, lies Assateague Island, a National Seashore shared with Maryland, where wild ponies graze. Virginia Beach leaves its crowds on the boardwalk and follows its quest for seclusion down among the cypress lagoons that lead on to the sea.

In the Virginia Piedmont, tobacco has ruled the fertile land for more than 300 years, spreading northward from the North Carolina border and pointing toward the falls of the Potomac. The marshes of the Eastern Shore had offered little

hope to those who trusted the earth for their living, so pioneers trekked westward—using the James and Rappahannock rivers to guide them—to a forest wilderness, then axed the trees and sprinkled the Piedmont with farms. Upon it, Thomas Jefferson built Monticello amidst the tobacco and wheat fields of Charlottesville, the Confederacy flew the stars and bars above its capitol at Richmond, and Robert E. Lee rode sadly amongst the peach blossoms of Appomattox to lay down his sword and end the War Between the States.

The Piedmont plateau of North Carolina falls out of the Blue Ridge Divide and moves past Raleigh toward the Atlantic, laced by the Pee Dee, Roanoke, and Catawba rivers. The Uwharrie Mountains, once regal at 20,000 feet, now are merely mounds beneath the woodlands. For time has not been kind to the Uwharries, chiseling and sanding them down to less than 1,000 feet. As North Carolina flattens out to meet the Atlantic, its fields surrender cotton, tobacco, and peanuts. In the Piedmont, the winds frolic through meadows thick with grain, and along the coast, commercial fishing vessels crowd into the quaint harbors of Beaufort, Wilmington, and Morehead City, architectural remnants of colonial seafaring days.

The Outer Banks stand alone. On the northern tip, at Kitty Hawk, where the sands were soft, the Wright brothers, Orville and Wilbur, took an engine and a wooden crate and made an airplane, just beyond Jockey's Ridge, where hang gliders still play with the winds. These outer islands of North Carolina are restless, always moving uneasily, the graveyard of the Atlantic. For centuries they have been battered by an ill-tempered sea. On the far side of the dunes, twisted wooden skeletons poke their broken ribs out of the surf, shipwrecks that the sea had claimed, then tossed ashore, never quite buried, never quite free from the sand that is their tomb. The shoals off Cape Hatteras, shallow and grim, lie in wait, a vicious trap that gives no warning in a maddened Atlantic. For 2,000 ships, the beacon from the cape's lighthouse beamed in vain. Sadness rides with the winds of the Outer Banks. Loneliness is one neighbor who hasn't left.

The Atlantic beaches curve southward to the coast and the Up Country of South Carolina, sand and palmetto that separate Little River and Tybee Sound almost 200 miles away. Charleston is the grande dame of the Low Country coast, down along Oyster Point, where the Ashley and Cooper rivers meet to form the Atlantic Ocean, or so the bluebloods say. Tea olives, banana shrubs, thornless roses, and Confederate jasmine grow in gardens behind colonial walls of stone and iron. The whole countryside slips beneath aged oaks, their branches webbed with Spanish moss, and hangs onto the marshes that step warily out into the black, stained surface of the salt water.

The coastline of South Carolina is rooted with clumps of myrtles and yaupon that bend landward in the Atlantic winds, pointing back toward pine groves and dark lagoons brightened by water lilies and blue hyacinths. The Grand Strand is a frail ladyfinger of sand that runs recklessly from Myrtle Beach to Georgetown, tying together the lazy fishing villages of Murrells Inlet and Pawleys Island, where the salt marshes befriend the ocean.

In 1663, Captain William Hilton sailed toward the beaches of South Carolina and wrote in the log of his ship: "Facing the sea, it is most pines, tall and good. The ayr is clean and sweet; the land passing pleasant . . . the goodliest, best and frutefullest ile ever was seen." Upon those islands—Hilton Head and Kiawah—men have built their resorts, and golf balls now nestle amongst the sand dollars.

When George Washington rode into the Low Country in 1791, he wrote of its "sand and pine barrens," explaining that "a perfect sameness seems to run through all the rest of the country." In time, peach orchards, cotton patches, and tobacco fields would blanket the pine belt uplands.

Long ago, ships sailed with rice and indigo from Georgetown, perched on Winyah Bay. The fields were rich and flooded by the Pee Dee, Sampit, Waccamaw, and Black rivers. But along the coastal swamp, indigo died as a cash crop after the Revolution, and long-fibered sea island cotton seeds were imported from the Bahamas. French silk mills stood ready to buy the crops before they were ever even planted. Upon the Sand Hills surrounding Columbia, blackjack oak and scrub pines are knotted together around flatland bald patches. Melons, tomatoes, and pecan orchards cover ground that was once white with cotton, back before the boll weevil broke both the farmer and his land. That soil, always washing away, has finally been lined with rows of California peas, Tennessee corn, Texas oats, white Dutch clover, Jerusalem artichokes, and Russian sunflowers. Man is fighting to heal his mistakes.

Down in the Georgia Piedmont, between Columbus and Macon, the land suffered the same fate. Before the turn of the century, cotton sapped the soil, and erosion left deep ugly scars in farmland that had been abused. Much of it would become pasture for horses and cattle. But back in the azalea and dogwood ravines, too deep for either man or sawmill to deface, nestles a tiny pocket of Appalachia creased with valleys that have developed what may be the largest number of plant species in the world. Some would feel more at home in the tropics, and others deserve to be out in the arid Southwest. Yet they live in harmony, outcasts in a land that didn't desert them.

The Georgia Piedmont tumbles eastward past great fields of tobacco and peanuts toward the Golden Isles, preserved through so many years by poverty and neglect, shattered by the sounds of war, reshaped at last by the influence of money. Sea Island, a playground for the rich, is separated from the mainland by the storied Marshes of Glynn. St. Simons is at rest beneath its lighthouse, guarded, as always, by the guns of Fort Frederica, a National Monument.

Just inland, Georgia is blessed—or cursed—with the Okefenokee Swamp, once described to me as "one of the quietest, most peaceful places on earth, especially about sundown." The Okefenokee unfolds below Waycross, gripped by lily pads and water lilies and sawgrass that turns brown, out among the cypresses that rise up starkly from a peat bog that, long ago, was part of the ocean floor. Springs feed the swampland. Boat trails cut through its 412,000 acres. And the blue herons, pileated woodpeckers, the white and wood ibis, and red-shouldered hawks are always on the move. It's never wise to hang around too long within reach of the bear,

Overleaf– NEW RIVER VALLEY, BLUE RIDGE PARKWAY / NORTH CAROLINA

RHODODENDRON IN SUNSET, BLUE RIDGE PARKWAY / VIRGINIA

bobcat, and 'gator, back in that unruly vestige of real estate that can be neither conquered nor civilized.

The Appalachian Mountains have always been the cornerstone of the South, ascending from the Virginias and North Carolina, hiking westward into Kentucky and Tennessee, and knifing down at last into the burly northern heights of Alabama and Georgia. They have long seemed aloof to me, proud, and maybe even haughty. I have often wondered if they looked upon man as an intruder—lost or just passing through—seldom paying much attention when he arrives and never missing him at all when he's gone.

Sweeping away from the slopes of the Blue Ridge in far western Virginia, rolling on down to the foothills of the Alleghenies, is Shenandoah, a valley and a river, whose landscape is dotted with the stone barns, split-rail fences, and gray, weathered cabins of settlers who dared journey beyond a mountain wall to find unspoiled farmland. The Indians quietly referred to the Shenandoah as "the daughter of the stars," there amidst the honeysuckle and Scotch broom that clung to those hillsides of hickory, hemlock, and birch.

A haze wrapped itself like a soft white gauze across the meadows the day I followed the bloody footsteps of Robert E. Lee, Stonewall Jackson, and Philip Sheridan across this valley, a valley too beautiful for battle, but one that had heard the cries of the dying as it changed hands 72 times during the Civil War. The smoke of powdered gunfire must have looked much like the haze that seized the northern funnel of the Shenandoah that morning, as I found myself among the apple blossoms of Winchester. They smelled of spring and peace, and lay against the sky like pink lace. The shadows of seven natural chimneys fell to the earth near Mount Solon, needles against the sun, ragged beneath ramparts that rose tall and defiant as the walls of a medieval castle. Once they had been labeled "The Cyclopean Towers," so reminiscent of the place that sheltered the mythological Cyclopes when they weren't out making thunderbolts for Zeus, or so I was told. Legends grow as often and as tall as the pines in Shenandoah.

We drove southward down the Blue Ridge Parkway, a paved tightrope that runs across the spine of the high country from Waynesboro, Virginia, to Cherokee, North Carolina. The mountains echoed the hardship of those who had transferred their tribulations to the names of the peaks that jutted up before us: Poor, Purgatory, Devil's Backbone.

The Blue Ridge Parkway leads on into the highlands of North Carolina, where old-time mountaineers found it virtually impossible to haul a load of corn over bad roads and rugged terrain. Besides, they discovered that a bushel of corn only sold for $1.50, while a bushel of distilled corn brought $53. So the high-country farmers became moonshiners, and the land brought them a wealth that they never expected. Most of the time it wasn't much. From cornshucks they wove dolls, fashioned rugs and scrub mops, and braided harnesses for mules. From river cane and split oak came baskets. And cowhide was used for shoes, vests, hats, chair bottoms, and even hinges for wooden doors.

Sometimes, however, the land gave more than it promised. In 1799, a 12-year-old boy stumbled across a 17-pound gold nugget near Concord. Having no idea what it was, his family used it as a doorstop for three years, finally selling it for $3.50. Not long afterward, one New York journalist reported he saw "at least one thousand persons at work panning for gold along the banks of Meadow Creek." Within 30 years, they had shoveled more than $10 million worth of the precious metal out of those mountains.

Left– ROCK BRIDGE, RED RIVER GORGE / KENTUCKY

Right– NATURAL BRIDGE / ALABAMA

When Christian Reid gazed out upon the peaks of North Carolina's Blue Ridge in 1876, he prayed, ''Dear Lord, I thank Thee for this, Thy gift, the land of sky.'' He had been smitten by the mountain laurel, rhododendron, and flame azaleas that rose up, as a velvet cloak of red, from the great granite backbone. Above him climbed Mount Mitchell, at 6,684 feet the highest peak east of the Mississippi River, and around him loomed the broad shoulders of the Great Smokies, the Blacks, and the Nantahalas, with more than 45 peaks stretching up toward the clouds at 6,000 feet.

On the western rim of the North Carolina high country, above Asheville, hang gliders dive for the wind that boils up alongside Grandfather Mountain. A rocky trail snakes down past crags and foliage to the Linville Gorge Wilderness Area, and the hardwood thickets of the Pisgah National Forest shut out the sun. In winter, snow ventures back into the ridges, dancing among ashen timber and sitting upon limbs that have been coldly deserted by their leaves. Some of it is even manmade. Boone, Blowing Rock, and Banner Elk find their riches on the slopes of the land as skis leave wayward tracks down mountains whose timbered walls have, at last, been conquered.

The Blue Ridge withers away in the northwest corner of South Carolina, with Sassafras Mountain the last granite outcropping to wedge itself into the red clay plateau. Table Rock and Caesar's Head drop sharply, the outer edges of a high country that has nowhere else to go. It was upon the summit of King's Mountain, near York, that British troops lost their fragile hold on South Carolina soil. The highlands fade quickly. They seem lost and out of place in a land that feels infinitely more comfortable with the sea.

Appalachia for years formed a dense barrier that denied early settlers a chance to journey inland to uncrowded land.

The high country of eastern Kentucky was virtually impregnable until 1775, when Daniel Boone and his men eased through the Cumberland Gap; and cleared a passage west for the Wilderness Road. Boone knew the mountains about as well as anyone, and he called this ''the most extraordinary country on which the sun has ever shone.''

The Breaks of Kentucky, outside Elkhorn City, slash their way down canyon walls that drop 1,600 feet from the Towers to the Russell Fork of the Big Sandy River, the largest gorge east of the Mississippi. Some call it the Grand Canyon of the South. Not far away is Hazard's Lilley Cornett Woods, holding within it the last remnant of a prehistoric forest—the Mixed Mesophytic—an untrammeled survivor that has successfully dodged the imprint of civilization. Beneath the earth, encompassing 51,000 acres is, as one old-timer said in awe, ''the greatest cave that ever was.'' The famed evangelist Billy Sunday once crawled out of Cave City's Mammoth Cave and explained, ''I felt smaller today than I ever did in my life, for I've just returned from exploring caverns that God has scooped out underneath the green hills of Kentucky.'' Near Corbin, Cumberland Falls roars through the forest, thunder without ceasing, a drumroll of sound that hasn't been silenced for more than 30 million years. It plunges for 68 feet, a broad skirt of water that fans out for 150 feet, the largest waterfall east of the Rockies and south of Niagara. At night, the cascading mist is a mirror for the moonlight, and a curious moonbow rises up out of the falls, a spectre in the darkness.

Tennessee hides its legends within the Great Smoky Mountains, cloaked by a thin will-o-the-wisp mist that entangles itself around the muscled peaks of a fragile highland. The Cherokee Indians know why the haze came. The chiefs from two tribes smoked the pipe of peace, then argued and fought for seven days and nights. The Great Spirit wasn't

pleased and turned the old men into gray flowers called Indian pipes, and he made them grow wherever friends have quarreled. He made the smoke of the pipe hang over the mountains until all people learned to live in peace.

Great Smoky Mountains National Park, spilling from North Carolina into Tennessee, covers 800 square miles with wizened peaks that have been watching over Appalachia for more than 200 million years. The slopes are quilted with wild flowers. Pine, oak, hemlock, and yellow poplar hug to the hideaway refuge for white-tailed deer, ruffed grouse, and Russian boar. The ridges are so steep, it is said, that farmers once climbed up mountainsides across the narrow valley from their gardens and blasted seeds into the ground with shotguns. The summers find shade. October's frosts paint the leaves of sweet gum and sumac purple, fire cherry and hawthorn red, persimmon and butternut yellow. Winter is the gray time of year. Snow. Pale skies. Trees that have undressed for the cold.

More than 1,300 different kinds of flowering plants run rampant in those highlands. In the late 1700s, William Bartram rode into the Smokies and wrote of the azaleas, ''The clusters of the blossoms cover the shrubs in such incredible profusion on the hillsides that . . . we were alarmed with apprehension of the hill being on fire.'' Among the hardwood forests, mountain laurel and rhododendron remain as the bramble brush of the high country, so thick and tangled that old settlers called them ''hells.''

The Appalachian ridge crawls southward past Knoxville to Chattanooga's Lookout Mountain—leaning into Georgia—where North and South fought their Battle Above the Clouds, 1,700 feet above the Moccasin Bend of the Tennessee River, above Chickamauga Creek, known as ''the river of blood.'' The Georgia mountains are bound in a solitude that comes when no one disturbs a land far from the beaten path. For it has been a long time since greed elbowed its way into the foothills of Dahlonega. The gold in its red clay afflicted men. It was as if someone had sprinkled the rivers and hillsides with tiny grains of gold from a huge salt shaker, tough to find, tougher to hold. From 1828 to 1838, the U.S. Mint at Dahlonega fashioned 1,378,710 coins worth more than $6.1 million from those tiny specks in the clay.

Across the top of Georgia, broad meadows separate the hills. Lakes spread among the valleys, their fingers reaching back into hidden coves that once felt the footsteps and heard the drumbeats of the Civil War. Brasstown Bald climbs highest of all, more than 4,000 feet. Cloudland Canyon hides away a rich lead mine, or so the Cherokees said. Across the summit of Kennesaw Mountain came the army of Gen. William T. Sherman, as he lit the torch to Georgia. Tallulah Gorge plummets as though the earth had forgotten it, a 2,000-foot-deep gash that is tempered by the outpouring of five waterfalls. And the angry Chattooga River surges with whitewater fury, pounding the rock cliffs of its narrow canyons, threading the back-country needle of Appalachia. Just outside Atlanta stands Stone Mountain, the world's largest granite monolith, rising 825 feet above the plain. Into its face the ghostly images of the South's Confederate heritage have been carved: likenesses of Jefferson Davis, Stonewall Jackson, and

Robert E. Lee on horseback. The sculptures are 36 stories high, larger than the figures on Mount Rushmore and the Sphinx at Giza.

Westward, the highlands of north Alabama are sometimes a little mysterious, as though each nook and cranny conceals a world of its own. Old farmsteads spill across broad meadows that chain together the steep bulkhead of the Blue Ridge. DeSoto Falls, near Mentone, tumbles wildly for 80 feet, dropping in a cloud of spray down Little River Canyon, hanging desperately to the strong ridges of Lookout Mountain. Along the walls of the ravine are traces of ancient Indian cave shelters, raided by Hernando DeSoto when he searched for gold in the 1500s but found only heartache and the long way home.

Ragged canyonlands crease the upper brow of Alabama. Hurricane Creek Gorge, near Cullman, ambles amiably, almost lazily, along a clear, spring-fed stream that slices through the last foothills of Appalachia, lost beneath a thick umbrella of mountain laurel, hickory, and pine. Rock Bridge Canyon, outside Hackleburg, is nothing more than a forbidding rock and flora garden where boulders and strange formations were created eons ago by sliding, wayward glaciers. And the Dismals, an untamed and sunken forest misplaced among the mountains, is haunting, secreted behind sheer rock walls and stitched together with trees that don't belong, waterfalls, and tunnels that are staggered throughout the high country. The early settlers of Phil Campbell, Alabama, didn't trust the Dismals at all. The sanctuaries, it seemed, lit up and glowed at night. But the phenomenon is only the dismalites, tiny, turned-on, phosphorescent worms that climb the rocks and appear blue, like the stars, when it's pitch dark. They have never been found anywhere but in the Dismals, in the summertime, when it rains.

The western slopes of the South's high country climb down from the mountains and ease across a gentle rolling plain that flattens out as it finds kinship with the Mississippi River Valley. In Kentucky, old fields range beyond the stone fences of Lexington, topped with the broad leaves of burley, of air-cured Green River dark tobacco, and Western dark-fired leaf tobacco, the kind that winds up in snuff cans. In older times, it was not merely a cash crop, it was cash itself, regarded as legal tender. Why, 26 pounds of good tobacco could buy a pretty fast horse. And Kentucky has had its share of pretty fast horses. More than 20,000 of them—proud and pampered—graze upon pastures of bluegrass. Standardbreds trot the Red Mile in Lexington. Thoroughbreds run for the roses in Louisville's Kentucky Derby. They are millionaires, born under the sign of the dollar. Upon those rich pastures of Kentucky bluegrass, men put white plank fences around their legends. Horses have always been royalty here, at least for a mile and a quarter.

Cotton and tobacco once ruled rural Tennessee, but those crops have turned the meadows over to cattle and walking horses. Much of the old farmland now lies buried beneath lakes, created primarily when the Tennessee Valley Authority harnessed the rivers and transformed the state's economy from agriculture to industry. Some say Tennessee is the home

SPANISH MOSS ALONG SOUTH RIVER / NORTH CAROLINA

of the Great Lakes of the South: Chickamauga and Nickajack at Chattanooga. Fort Patrick Henry at Kingsport. Fort Loudin at Lenoir. Pickwick near Savannah. Percy Priest at Nashville. And, of course, the Land Between the Lakes (Kentucky and Barkley) is a patch of well-protected wilderness that drops out of Kentucky toward Paris, Tennessee.

In the southwestern corner of the state Memphis reigns over the part of the Mississippi where cotton is still king. Old Man River, the Mississippi itself, washes up on the muddy banks of Memphis, then churns on past levees and plantations on its somnolent journey to the sea at New Orleans. The whistle of the steamboat has faded, but barges hitch a ride and dodge the sandbars that lie in wait, sometimes treacherous, always a nuisance.

The western shoreline of the Mississippi nudges Arkansas, described by the Spanish explorer DeSoto as ''a fair and pleasant land.'' Peach orchards huddle together at the base of Red Lick Mountain near Clarksville. The Wiederkehr vineyards drape themselves around the winemaking hamlet of Altus. Throughout Arkansas, the pine forests and mountains hold such bass fishing kingdoms as Bull Shoals, Beaver Lake, Greer's Ferry, Nimrod, Lake Ouachita, and Dardanelle. At Gulpha Gorge, outside Hot Springs, gray boulders hang onto the mountainside like bricks from a wind-chiseled fireplace, embroidered by the delicate pink lady slipper and spider flower, sheltered by a dense oak and hickory forest. Down in the flatlands, below Little Rock, the power of cotton has at last wilted on the vine. Rice fields slosh across the Grand Prairie around Stuttgart, as ducks come winging through the dawn and men who don't trust nature create their own floods, making money from the wet, seemingly worthless plain that God gave them.

Arkansas' hill country lies northward. We found a scrapbook of hopes and disappointments in the Boston Mountains, all written on the weathered sidings of abandoned towns that struggled for a while, then gave up the ghost. In Winslow, an old-timer told me that Satan himself could feel right at home at Devil's Den State Park. When early-day settlers stumbled across that dragon-mouthed cavern, they were convinced that they had found the final resting place of the evil old archangel. The Ozark Mountains stand tall, and the land is insolent and harsh, a hard-scrabble slice of plow-scarred rocks and unmarked graves among the scrub oaks. The mountains dared man to survive, and he cursed the beauty that he revered. The Buffalo River brings relief to the rugged, isolated terrain, twisting along massive rock cliffs that cluster across the top of Arkansas, moving past the old abandoned zinc mining country around Yellville, and flowing on to Ponca's Lost Valley, sealed off by a natural bridge that ties the stark limestone bluffs to a gentle, sloping hillside. It hides at the end of a small tunnel that winds like a corkscrew between sheer cliffs for nearly a mile to the cave of Crystal Springs, leading on to Clark Creek and a ravine that is dotted, like a well-used pincushion, with tiny caves. Not far away, the valley abruptly ends, and Crystal Eden Falls pours from a little cavern, splashing downward over a sandstone draw to the creek, 200 feet below. The sun touches the water, and the water blesses the earth, and, for a mo-

ment, the Ozarks don't feel so harsh anymore.

The muddy, slow-moving Mississippi River leaves Arkansas behind and ambles toward the Gulf of Mexico, clutching the western edge of Louisiana firmly in its grasp. It has long been the major highway for the South to ship its crops to the market center of New Orleans, heavy laden with flatboats and keelboats of tobacco and cotton, of rice and sugar cane from the moist soil of Louisiana itself. The abundance of river traffic once prompted Thomas Jefferson to say, ''The position of New Orleans certainly destines it to be the greatest city the world has ever seen.'' Today New Orleans leads North American ports in tonnage handled annually, ahead of New York and Houston.

Louisiana has always depended on its waterways, especially back among the live oak illusions of its Cajun country, that strange blend of French, Indian, Spanish, and Creole culture that blossoms amongst the swamps and levees below Lafayette and Baton Rouge. The bayous of south Louisiana curl through palmetto and cypress knees, cast upon the land like the thin, broken strands of a wind-blown spider web, wet, brackish roadways for log pirogues that, Cajuns swear, can ride on a heavy dew. Bayou Teche, sliding past New Iberia, is the most majestic of all, a place created, the Indians say, by the writhing of a huge silver snake that wore deep grooves in the soft, decaying dirt, then waited for the water to fill the cuts where it had passed by. The earth continually shifts down where alligator grass and salt cane form a walking prairie across the marshlands. Earthen levees push back the sea, and gnarled oaks bitterly fight for life upon the

MISSISSIPPI RIVER AT NATCHEZ / MISSISSIPPI

chênières, ridges of sand on a barrier beach where salt water slowly and ultimately sucks the life away, leaving the trees to lean like gray, shrunken crosses upon the sands that doomed them.

The pines of Louisiana crowd the sandhills around Shreveport, leading southeast to the Kisatchie National Forest and the logging industry of Winnfield. Monroe found itself rooted to a vast pool of natural gas. And Lake Charles acquired wealth from oil and gas that lingered deep beneath the tides of the Gulf. The old crops faded, and columned mansions became rotting, abandoned hulks, keeping watch over a land that plantation lords had owned and lost.

Behind the chênières, the moss-woven innards of the Atchafalaya Swamp are home for fish and wildlife. One of America's last great river swamps, the Atchafalaya seethes with crawfish; it floods when it loses its temper. The Atchafalaya, ranging from Lafayette to Morgan City, is unpredictable and fickle. Old men live back in the swamp, and they've never owned automobiles. No need to, they say. ''There ain't no roads back in there.'' A pirogue gets them around just fine. One of them said of the Atchafalaya: ''Take almost any acre of land you want, and—during a single year—you can trap otter, raccoon, mink, oppossum, skunk, and nutria on it. You can hunt deer, rabbit, squirrel, woodcock, or ducks on it. And you can catch bass, perch, catfish, sacalait, buffalo, and crawfish on it. It just depends on whether that acre is wet or dry.''

Beyond the eastern banks of the Mississippi River lies a land where plantation owners and sharecroppers alike based their lone hope on the success of the cotton boll. Since 1917, the world's largest long staple cotton market has been tucked away in downtown Greenwood, Mississippi. And the first cotton crop in the world produced entirely by machinery came out of Mississippi's Coahoma County. Now rice, corn, pecans, wheat, oats, and soybeans—even oil and gas wells—occupy that delta dirt where cotton no longer is royalty.

Mississippi is a land that has known the best of times and the worst. Antebellum millionaires built the white-columned mansions of Natchez beneath magnolias and on the front doorstep of Old Man River. Civil War gunfire splintered the pineland thickets of Tupelo and brought starvation to the steep bluffs of Vicksburg.

Sawmill towns like Hattiesburg have been thrust into Mississippi's long leaf pine belt, which wraps itself in the DeSoto National Forest. And Columbus surrounds the grandeur of its antique homes with the Tombigbee National Forest. Pine and hardwood knit the states of the South with a bond as common as grits and redeye gravy. Nowhere is the beauty of the woodland more prevalent than along the Natchez Trace Parkway as it rambles through Tennessee and Mississippi. From the tracks of wild animals it originally came, a pathway through canebrakes and unruffled meadows, a vital link in the early 1800s between Nashville and Natchez. The road through the wilderness has been eulogized in pavement by the National Park Service, a 306-mile memorial to the men and women who carted their hopes, dreams, and fears westward. The parkway doesn't pretend to travel the exact route of the Natchez Trace, but it never strays far

from that early path, paralleling at times the historic ruts that wagon wheels and horses' hooves trampled deep into the tender loess soil.

The forests are a dark shelter upon the face of Mississippi. The Gulf Coast is free and open, reaching past its own beach toward the dunes, low marsh grass, and sea oats of Ship Island. Along with the isles of Horn, Cat, and Petit Bois, Ship Island is an unadorned link in the Gulf Islands National Seashore chain, where the ruins of Fort Massachusetts are the last sentry, a wasted sentry, built in 1856 to protect the coast from a Spanish invasion that never came. The sands of the Gulf drift eastward, a barefoot world where there's a beach for every mood. Dauphin Island is the orphan scape of Alabama, in the mouth of Mobile Bay, wrapped in a warm, wrinkled blanket of solitude, a place to be lonely, to laugh, to catch the sun that no one ever holds for long.

From the coves and inlets of its chiseled coastline, Alabama stretches northward into the black agricultural soil of its midlands, where peanut vines cover the fields of Dothan, primarily because George Washington Carver discovered that the peanut could be a commercially profitable crop in soil that had been depleted by planting too much cotton and was plagued by too many boll weevils. Only the antebellum homes of Montgomery reflect the heritage of cotton. The land had to find its fortune from some other source. In time, it did. Around the foothills that one day would harbor Birmingham, Creek Indians used iron ore for war paint. That hematite intrigued the white man, drawing him into the bowl between the mountains where he found a valley of limestone, buttressed on one side by a massive hill of red iron ore and on the other by a mighty coal range. It turned out to be the only place in the world where the three ingredients for making steel are in such close proximity. Soon the furnaces of Birmingham fired Alabama with a new kind of wealth, but wealth taken, as always, from the goodness of the land.

The northern crest of Florida weds itself to the piney woods of lower Alabama, a rural panhandle that is checkered with farms and weather-beaten cabins. It exudes a down-home kind of charm, mirrored by the Suwannee, the river Stephen Foster wrote about but never saw. In central Florida, cattle graze the ranges of Kissimmee, just as they have ever since Ponce de Leon first brought cows ashore in 1521. There amidst the palms, the sun nurtures citrus crops that grow thick and ripe in an eden that is forever drenched by the artificial rains of irrigation. More oranges are grown on the ridge of Polk County alone, for example, than in any other state. And sugar cane nails its tall stalks to the black dirt surrounding Lake Okeechobee, just beyond the seemingly endless fields of beans and corn.

On the southern tip of Florida the Everglades tremble, a land of 'gators and gardens, trapped amidst moss and quicksand, wallowing in bogs and mangrove thickets. For some, the swamps are pristine, a world that captures the holy essence of life in chaos and transition. The fragile river of grass sprawls over 5,000 square miles, wild and shallow, its nearly 1.4 million acres protected by the National Park Service. One day an airboat skimmed the sawgrass, carrying me back into the mysterious heart of the mangrove and cypress swamp-

land, back where alligators lie like logs in the sun, deer run free, panthers prowl, bears stalk, and the bald eagle is among the 326 species of birds that circle overhead. I sped past egrets and the roseate spoonbills, huge pink birds with crimson splashes, creatures we almost lost because man slaughtered them to make feathered plumes for women's hats. At times, the water was barely two inches deep beneath the boat as it barreled down narrow sloughs, cutting around the hammocks, islands of trees without soil. An otter chased a frog. A deer scooted back on dry land with suspicious eyes. An ibis strutted into the green shadows. The swamp is beautiful, I said. Yes, I was told, but then, so is a snake.

Florida's coast has long been the land of great expectations. Facing the Atlantic, eight flags have flown above Fernandina Beach, waving proudly over the sweep of salt marshes and mud flats that are left naked when tidal waters sneak away into the night. Amelia Island has become a resort that blends luxury into oak, palmetto, and sunken forests that creep to the feet of dunes and bend before the spray of ocean winds. Upon the hard-packed beaches of Daytona and Ormand, Fred Marriott drove his famed Stanley Steamer Rocket to a world record of 127.6 miles an hour, piloting the first auto to ever travel faster than two miles a minute. A scientific magazine of the day proclaimed that such speeds "caused harmful chemical reactions in the body, producing temporary insanity." Thus was born the term "speed demon." From the sands of Cape Canaveral, other rockets climbed to the moon and beyond, while not far away, upon the shallow Indian River, brown pelicans nest safely in the first national wildlife refuge ever established in America. Miami has built huge hotels and land-grabbing condominiums atop the sands where man once walked, then tried to create his own beaches—only to see them destroyed by the sea.

Somewhere just south of the Florida Keys, the Atlantic and the Gulf of Mexico become as one, out where the tarpon explode from turquoise waters and sailfish cut into an alley that bears their name. Coral reefs bare their beauty at John Pennekamp, the nation's first underwater park. Birds rise in great winged curtains, filling the sky and blotting out a sur-

Left– TUPELO AND CYPRESS ALONG SUWANNEE RIVER / GEORGIA

Above– BALD CYPRESS, BAYOU GRAND / LOUISIANA

prised sun above the Florida Bay rookeries of Tavernier. And tiny key deer, each the size of a collie dog, bounce into the brush, sliding past the bored white herons of Big Pine Key.

The Gulf shovels white sands up on the west coast. Crescent-shaped Sanibel and Captiva islands, off Fort Myers, are known worldwide for the shells that are deposited on their beaches. They are the last holdouts: a land where seashells and driftwood still outnumber the footprints. Marco Island has been overrun by tourists and developers. And up along the coast of Florida's panhandle drift the sands of the Miracle Strip, crisp, the texture of new-fallen snow, linked by the dunes of Panama City, Destin, Fort Walton Beach, and Pensacola. The sands. They are solitude or soaked with suntan lotion. They hear the lonely cry of a seagull or the white-knuckled scream of a roller coaster. They are at peace or in panic. Across the kindly waters of Escambia Bay, Pensacola Beach is the mute legacy of Spanish soldiers who trekked upon the sands in 1559 and tried to build a future. But, alas, a hurricane chased them away. Now, only the hollow eyes of crumbling Fort Pickens remain, the hermit of the dunes.

I have always felt a close kinship with the South. It is a place where I have lost myself for a while and felt a little sad when I found my way out again. The mountains, no matter how aloof, could make me forget my troubles. Or the oceans, no matter how angry, could wash them away. Somewhere through the years, the South became a friend, or perhaps it has always been family. Its isolation became my escape, the solitude my home. The land was good to the South. It provided opportunity, and it promised wealth. And sometimes, the beauty and the sanctity of the land were the only rewards it had to offer. Most times, that was enough.

Above– FALL CREEK LAKE, FALL CREEK FALLS STATE PARK / TENNESSEE

Right– DAWN, CADES COVE, GREAT SMOKY MOUNTAINS NATIONAL PARK / TENNESSEE

Left– NEW RIVER GORGE, GRANDVIEW STATE PARK / WEST VIRGINIA

Right– CEDAR ON LEDGE RIM, MAGAZINE MOUNTAIN / ARKANSAS

Left– CUMBERLAND FALLS STATE PARK / KENTUCKY

Below– DOGWOOD, TABLE ROCK STATE PARK / SOUTH CAROLINA

Top– PINNACLE OVERLOOK, CUMBERLAND GAP NATIONAL
HISTORIC PARK / TENNESSEE-KENTUCKY-VIRGINIA

Bottom– CASH LAKE, DESOTO STATE PARK / ALABAMA

Left– NATIVE GRASSES, PEA RIDGE NATIONAL MILITARY PARK / ARKANSAS

Above– SEA OATS, SANIBEL ISLAND / FLORIDA

Left– COCO PALMS, KEY WEST / FLORIDA

Right– POND CYPRESS AND LILY PADS, COOKS HAMMOCK / FLORIDA

CORNFIELD EDGE / IOWA

The Heartland

Power from the Earth Abundant

BY HARVEY C. JACOBS

IN THE 1920s THE INDIANAPOLIS *NEWS* EMPLOYED A resident poet named William Herschell. Herschell wrote mostly regional verse, and he was assured everlasting fame in Indiana by a poem he called "Ain't God Good to Indiana?" He could have written it for the whole Heartland. In this fertile, mineral-rich land live 59 million people, whose ancestors are drawn from every quadrant of the globe. In spite of periodic wars, depressions, floods, and dust storms, the people here have lived well.

Historian Walter Havighurst said the Heartland was "massed with power and purpose." Much of the power came from the land. The purpose came from the people, many of whom broke out of the older eastern and southern colonies in the early 1800s to start new lives. They were responding to the lure of new land, which they hoped would be more fertile than the stony shelves of New England from which many of them came. They also came on horseback and in creaky wagons from the South, following the Wilderness Road through the Cumberland Gap.

When my great-great-grandfather Sam Jacobs was mus-

tered out of the Revolutionary Army, he joined the motley caravan of Virginians heading for what was to become the Northwest Territory. He paused in Ohio, where family legend has it he met a relative named John Chapman, better known as Johnny Appleseed. Chapman, an itinerant peddler-missionary of the early 1800s, traveled much of the Heartland planting appleseeds. Grandfather Sam moved on into Indiana. It was the kind of westward movement that was typical of the time.

My mother's parents, Vandiviers and Ragsdales, came to Indiana by another route, through Kentucky. I once asked Grandfather Ragsdale why his family chose central Indiana as the best place to stake their claims.

"Because they found so many sugar maple trees," he explained. "They knew that the land was fertile wherever the sugar trees grow."

In a reminiscent mood, he said, "I was just a tiny kid, but I remember that the forests were so dense here that you couldn't drive a wagon through. You could make it on horseback, but the men cut the trees out there"—he pointed toward

Illinois
Indiana
Iowa
Kansas
Michigan
Minnesota
Missouri
Nebraska
North Dakota
Ohio
South Dakota
Wisconsin

the fields of green corn rustling in the July breeze—"so they could get the wagons through."

Today, I still have 19 acres of the land from the original claims, and it's almost as well-forested with maple trees as it was when Grandfather's parents settled here. Perhaps I should say it has been "reforested," because through the years much of the timber has been harvested since the original settlement in the 1840s.

These wooded centerpieces still exist across the Heartland. Around them are fields of corn and wheat, ordered rows of soybeans, and peaceful pastures where cattle graze. Many farmers are glad they have saved their woodlots; wood stoves and fireplaces have made a comeback as alternative energy sources.

The face of the Heartland is mostly open and green. An Ohio or Illinois farmer set down in New England would say, "I'm too hemmed in." In the Southwest he might say: "Yes, I can see forever here, but the land's no good unless it can grow corn." A Texan seeing Iowa for the first time, however, might respond: "Those cornfields don't offer much variety."

The Heartland does not flaunt an imperious countenance. The land rolls along on flats and knolls. Small streams and rivers curl like commas around the fertile bottoms. The once-dense forests are preserved mostly in state and national forests—of which there are many—and by a few conservationist owners who value maple, oak, ash, and poplar more than they value annual cash crops.

The woodlands—public and private—are symbols of historical change. In the 1830s and 1840s the axe preceded the plow. Settlers helped each other "roll" the logs and build their houses. Then, woodcutters turned themselves into farmers. The farmers planted corn and clover, fenced the fields for hogs and cattle, and sent their produce into the towns and cities. A new class of workers in the small towns processed the produce and provided services to the countryside. By the mid-1920s, when my 85-year-old grandfather was reminiscing about the changes he had seen, the Heartland had become a prospering region serviced by thousands of small towns.

Small-town America found its voice and image in Sinclair

Lewis's *Main Street*. "This is America," he wrote. "Main Street is the continuation of Main Streets everywhere." His hometown was in the Heartland—Sauk Centre, Minnesota. In spite of the parochialism dramatized in his famous novel, the small town became the model setting for achieving the Good Life in America. The towns were small enough and the farm communities intimate enough that the "Howdies" and the "Hellos" were spontaneous. Friendliness and neighborliness carried over from the log-rollings.

The pioneer tradition of equality of sacrifice between husband and wife was carried forward, too. In the late 1920s the *Ladies Home Journal* published a lengthy article by an anonymous farm wife who summed up her "modern" role: "Partnership from the ground up means the farm is *ours*. Our land is ours, the home is ours, and all the work we put into improvements is ours. When you step outside your door, you have your own good brown earth and green grass under your feet. Nothing can take it away from us as long as we pay the taxes."

The American family flourished in such an environment. Reflecting upon his Kansas roots, President Dwight D. Eisenhower summed up: "All in all, we were a cheerful and vital family. Our pleasures were simple, but we had plenty of fresh air, exercise, and companionship. We would have

been insulted had anyone offered us charity."

Into this pastoral framework, the twentieth century gradually unfolded its panorama of grain elevators, steel mills, automobile factories, breweries, and coalfields. A way of life was transformed by mechanization into an integrated system for filling the nation's food basket. Yet, traced to their roots, the industrial intrusions grew mostly out of the needs of a burgeoning agriculture and a dispersed rural population. The inventors and innovators even came from the small towns and farms. Henry Ford, Harvey Firestone, Wilbur and Orville Wright, Thomas Edison, George Washington Carver— the list could go on—are only a few who came from the Heartland states.

The base on which this half rural, half industrial society rests has its origins millions of years ago. Geologists say that at least four Arctic glaciers, formed by accumulated winter snows that survived the summer sun for thousands of years, pushed southward to cover almost half of North America. The last, the Wisconsin glacier, retreated about 11,000 years ago. It had a special affinity for the Heartland states.

It rasped away the craggy mountains, dug new valleys, stripped the soil to bedrock in some places, and leveled fertile soil in others. It shifted and, in some cases, exposed rich veins of ore and minerals. Myriad lakes were scooped out,

Overleaf–MITCHELL PASS, OREGON TRAIL, SCOTTS BLUFF NATIONAL MONUMENT / NEBRASKA

Left– NIOBRARA RIVER, AGATE FOSSIL BEDS NATIONAL MONUMENT / NEBRASKA

Below– OHIO RIVER AT POWHATAN POINT / OHIO

old rivers dammed and diverted to new channels. The glacier thrust its icy blade southward to level three-quarters of Ohio, Indiana, Illinois, and Missouri, then moved in an irregular northwestern line almost to the Canadian border in North Dakota, and pushed straight west to the mountains. The western mountains held back the ice, and from the breakup a rich crop of mountain glaciers was formed and joined together to create an ice cap connecting with the eastern continental glacier.

As the Wisconsin ice sheet retreated, it put the finishing touches on the Great Lakes and filled them with half the fresh water in the world. It heaped up a ridge on the northern shores, damming off the northern lowlands. The confined water, now under pressure, poured south and east to form new systems of drainage.

One of the pressure points was near where Toledo, Ohio, now stands. The water poured out of Lake Erie and made a channel to the Ohio River, reversing its flow and turning it toward the Mississippi River. The Wabash and Maumee rivers follow the same valley. This route later became the site of the Wabash and Erie Canal, between Toledo and Evansville, Indiana. The canal played an important role in opening northern Ohio and Indiana to development, although it was not a financial success.

Another Great Lakes outlet ran through the site of Chicago and followed the present courses of the Des Plaines and Illinois rivers to the Mississippi. The Illinois and Michigan Canal was dug in this valley in 1836–1838 to tie Lake Michigan to the Illinois River, thence to the Mississippi.

The Heartland has no ocean coastline, but water and waterways have been important to its development. Its eastern half is almost completely surrounded by navigable waters. A network of major rivers and their tributaries provided access to the unmapped frontiers and, later, became the arteries of communications and commerce. It was natural that so much of the Heartland's commerce should develop around the Great Lakes; ringing the lakes were trees for lumber, iron ore for steel, and coal for heating homes and fueling factories. Cleveland, Toledo, Detroit, Chicago, Milwaukee, and Duluth became port cities on America's "fourth seacoast."

The main artery of river transport, the Mississippi River, splices the whole nation together, draining 31 states and two Canadian provinces. Its watershed stretches from the Allegheny Mountains to the Rockies. Ironically, the Father of Waters does not carry as much water as the Ohio and is not as long as the Missouri. Its central location, however, gave it preeminence.

Two years after the Louisiana Purchase in 1803, President

Jefferson sent Zebulon Pike to explore the Upper Mississippi. Pike did not locate its source, but he came close. At its source—the clear waters of Lake Itasca in northern Minnesota—the Mississippi is 10 to 12 feet wide and two feet deep. It runs northward for a short span, then twists and turns toward the southeast. In its upper reaches, the river is not much different today from the time of Zebulon Pike. The country is still wild and rugged. The Arctic three-toed woodpecker nests in the Norway pines. The call of the loon is a sound out of the timeless silence of the forest. The bald eagle has a home hereabouts. Deer canter along the reed-rimmed stream; even a black bear now and then ventures into a sparse sunny clearing. Red-winged blackbirds flutter in the willows, and an occasional timber wolf passes through.

The thickets are almost prehistorically forbidding. The black spruce and tamarack crowd up to the stream's marshy rim. There are aspen, birch, alder, ash, and basswood. This is pristine wilderness opening occasionally into pastures and marshy swampland. The river takes at least 100 miles to set a steady course toward the Gulf of Mexico. It circles and meanders through wooded banks as dense as those first measured by Pike. Approaching the Twin Cities, Minneapolis and St. Paul, it collects itself between high bluffs, grows deeper and wider, and becomes navigable for commercial boats.

South of the Twin Cities, the first large tributaries enter the main stream to the Gulf of Mexico: the Des Moines, Minnesota, and Missouri rivers from the west, and the Illinois, Wisconsin, Chippewa, and St. Croix rivers from the east. The main stream plods along, forming and reforming backwater marshes and islands. These marshes have become a center of wildlife. The Upper Mississippi Wild Life and Fish Refuge, founded in 1924, contains 194,000 acres of river wetlands, beginning at Lake Pepin in Wisconsin and extending to Rock Island in Illinois. More than 3.5 million people visit it every year, making it the most popular wildlife refuge in the United States.

Beavers were reintroduced into the backwaters in the 1920s. Fish have multiplied in the shallow water, muskrats live by the mudbanks. Ducks use the river corridor as their migratory route. By October the bald eagles move in to search for wounded waterfowl. By December the eagles move out into the channel to find pools where the ice does not impede their fishing. As many as 700 eagles spend their winters along the Upper Mississippi.

As the river passes into Iowa and Illinois, the pastures along the banks are filled with cows and hogs. Fields of corn and soybeans flatten out the landscape and open up the view. Rocky bluffs highlight the banks, some of them rising to a height of 600 feet, forming great palisades of rugged beauty.

In Missouri the river has left its mark in the bluffs and in the limestone caverns. They were formed by groundwater holding carbon dioxide and organic acids, which ate into the limestone at its fracture lines. Mark Twain (Samuel Clemens), the riverboat pilot turned author, set some of his best stories in the caves along the Mississippi. Tom Sawyer and Becky Thatcher lost their way in the ''murky aisles'' winding from one underground room to another. In *The Adventures of Tom Sawyer,* they played hide-and-seek in the Drawing Room,

the Cathedral, and Aladdin's Palace.

The bluffs, caves, and limestone escarpments end at Cape Girardeau in southern Missouri. At Cairo, Illinois, the Father of Waters, in company with the Ohio River, forms a vast and restless floodplain reaching to New Orleans.

On its way to the Gulf, the Mississippi flows through 10 states, but it cradles the Heartland with special attention. Over the centuries the cycles of floods and drought have alternately washed away the soil and redeposited it in fertile fields and bottoms. At the peak of floods, the river's power is awesome.

Mark Twain, through one of his riverboat pilots, Uncle Mumford, has his say about man's feeble efforts to tame the Mississippi: ''There at Devil's Island, in the Upper River, they wanted the water to go one way, the water wanted to go another. So they put up a stone wall. But what does the river care for a stone wall? When it got ready, it just bulged through it.''

It is a restless river, continually creating new channels. Wherever driftwood lodges, there is the promise of a new sandbar. The sandbar becomes an island, but it may melt away in the press of the next floodwater. The waves chew constantly at the shores, forming new configurations.

In its wayward surge to the sea, the Mississippi touches the variegated cultures of the Scandinavian dairymen in Minnesota and Wisconsin and the diverse blend of European cultures represented among the settlers in Iowa, Illinois, and Missouri. Colorful legends were born in the steamboat days. Artists steamed its scenic lengths to paint what America really looked like. Note-reading composers and foot-stomping folk singers alike celebrated the river in song. Writers, most notably Twain, told the world about the river and the people who lived on and near it. The river itself became a setting for any and all with a desire to set themselves adrift.

On the pioneer maps Missouri was a crossroads. The dominant flow of the rivers was north to south, but the later settlers possessed the urge to ''Go West.'' Grandfather Sam Jacobs had six sons, two of whom responded to the spirit of adventure in the air. One found what he was seeking—free and fertile land—in Iowa, and his descendants are pillars of the community around Sigourney. The other followed the crowd to Missouri, where, around St. Louis and Independence, wagon trains were forming into caravans. He ended up in northern California, where again the descendants have their names on rural mailboxes today. The family movement was typical of the times.

The westward movers were mightily challenged by crossing the Mississippi River. If they could conquer that, some concluded, the remainder of the journey would surely be downhill.

The city of St. Louis has marked the gateway to the west with a 630-foot arch designed by the famous Finnish architect Eero Saarinen. An architectural marvel, it provides a panorama of the river and a westward view of the city. It is the symbol of the westward movement and a model for bringing the meaningful past into the present.

One of the early pioneer travelers, seeing Ohio, Indiana, and Illinois for the first time, sent a letter back to his Virginia family with this comment: ''You won't see any spectacular scenery here, but if you want to settle and grow things, there

FARM ROAD NEAR GALENA / ILLINOIS

is a fortune to be made.''

The Heartland has been growing things ever since, and the superficial observer may not sense the inner grandeur of the predominantly placid landscape. The New England poet Robert Frost once said the soil of Iowa looked ''good enough to eat.''

The Heartland is half agricultural and half industrial, but the cities grew out of the agriculture surrounding them. Today the huge crops of soybeans, corn, wheat, hogs, poultry, sheep, and cattle funnel into the city markets in awesome abundance. The process is industrialized of course, but the poetry remains in the green seas of corn and wheat and in the lush pastures. At night during the growing season those of us attuned to the cycle of the seasons can actually hear the corn growing to the accompaniment of a chorus of insects and night creatures.

Ohio, Michigan, Wisconsin, Illinois, and Indiana, all lying in the curving industrial corridor around the Great Lakes, are generally considered industrial. But they are also agricultural. Illinois, for example, produces more grain and legumes than Iowa, although Iowa leads all Heartland states in livestock production. The northern tier—Michigan, Wisconsin, and Minnesota—also produces food in abundance, in spite of a shorter growing season. Minnesota is third among the Heartland states in livestock production.

These three states are also ruggedly attractive, with their lakes, hills, and tall timber. Minnesota, the ''Land of 10,000 Lakes,'' lures visitors and sportsmen. The state actually has more than 15,000 lakes. Not far behind are Michigan with 11,000 and Wisconsin with 8,500. These states have soil that produces hay, orchards, and vineyards. The clover and alfalfa feed the dairy cattle, making the best milk and cheese in the land. Beneath much of the soil lie stone, gravel, granite, iron ore, and minerals.

This is timber country, too, providing the setting for the mythical lumberjack, Paul Bunyan. Paul was born across the border in Canada, but emigrated soon to Heartland lumber camps. His helper was Babe, the Blue Ox, who helped Paul build the Mississippi. She used the Great Lakes as her drinking trough. Kansas is flat, according to this folklore hero, because Paul hitched Babe to it and turned it over to make good corn and wheat land.

Kansas lore has it that in 1874 a farmer newly arrived from the Russian steppes reached down to grasp a handful of the

Left– ROCK FORMS, WISCONSIN DELLS / WISCONSIN

Above– BIG SPRING, CURRENT RIVER, OZARK NATIONAL SCENIC RIVERWAYS / MISSOURI

rich, black earth. Gazing across the flat prairie, he said, "In three years that ocean of grass will be transformed into an ocean of waving fields of grain."

The prophecy was fulfilled mostly because Mennonites from the Crimea brought seed wheat called Turkey Red. It was the beginning of making Kansas the nation's wheat capital. The state produces a fifth of the total crop in the United States.

Today, as in the beginning, the summer wind brings the wheat harvests, for the wind seems to blow the gold into the ripening wheat. The waves ripple toward infinity, swaying and twisting in a slow dance. When the wind rests and the heat settles, the wheat stands shimmering like a calm ocean in a summer sun. It's ready for the combines that gulp in the stalks and disgorge the straw in one place and the grains in another.

South Dakota produces grain, too, but mostly in the "east river" area set off by the Missouri River. Oats, flax, and hay also grow well. "West river" is cowboy and shepherd country, where flat ranches tilt up to the setting sun. Farther west the low mountains called the Black Hills nudge Wyoming. They are "black" because, viewed from the distant plain, their domed forests appear invitingly dark. Wild game thrives here.

The land was once the bottom of an inland sea, where subsequent glaciers ironed out plains and prairies, gouged tranquil lakes and rivers, and heaved up the Badlands, which were left rugged and raw, emulating a moonscape full of grandeur and mystery. The fossils they have given up document the world of dinosaurs and other prehistoric animals. This area is also the nation's largest supplier of gold.

Coming from the tree-covered Midwest, North Dakota's first settlers must have confronted the treeless tabletop west of the Red River with disappointment. From what would they build their houses?

Looking downward from the limitless sky, they saw the lush grasses—sod! The new settlers learned to slice and fit it into walls and roofs—from which the folk songs about "sod shanties"were born.

The settlers who moved on west and south, across the Missouri plateau, found trees: cottonwood, willow, elm, ash, birch, and more. Wherever they turned, the soil was fertile. Game was abundant. It still is. North Dakota has more wildlife refuges than any other state.

There is a near mystical quality to much of the Dakota landscape. Theodore Roosevelt discovered that quality in 1883 when he went there on a hunting trip. He became a Dakota cattleman and made North Dakota his second home. His description captures some of the appeal: "The grassy, scantily wooded bottoms through which the river flows are bounded by bare, jagged buttes; their fantastic shapes and sharp, steep edges throw the most curious shadows, under the cloudless glaring sky; and at evening I love to sit out in front of the hut and see their hard gray outlines gradually growing soft and purple as the flaming sunset by degrees softens and dies away."

Roosevelt was a rugged outdoorsman. He loved the challenge of weather, but the prairie winds often drove him to shelter. "Sometimes furious gales blow down from the north," he wrote, "driving before them the clouds of blinding snowdust, wrapping the mantle of death around every unsheltered being that faces this unshackled anger."

The unshackled anger of winter can be dangerous to both man and beast in much of the Heartland. The raw winds sweep ruthlessly across Kansas, for example, where even the Indians were impressed by those who could survive the wind. The Indian name for Kansas territory was *Kansa,* meaning "wind people." Snow sometimes clogs the highways of all the Heartland states. It isolates communities, causes power failures, and maroons thousands of persons who can't leave their homes until the snowplows get through.

Extreme and rapid weather changes test the adaptability of every inhabitant. "You don't like our weather?" we in Indiana say to out-of-state visitors. "Stay a couple of hours and it'll be different."

To persons depending upon favorable climate for harvests, this is high risk territory. But there are compensating assets. Water in the rivers and lakes makes the landscape beautiful; water from heaven makes it green and productive. Without its annual 40-inch rainfall, the Heartland could not have become the breadbasket of America.

There is also the challenge of making weather a partner. From the beginning, the settlers learned that the anger of the elements could be channeled. Like the sod, the weather could be used. Windmills were erected to harness the wind to drive the pumps to lift drinking water from the innards of the earth. When the growing season was too short for one strain of wheat, the farmers found another. When the floods flushed away the topsoil, dams and levees were put in place. When winds, along with drought, lifted the loose soil into blankets of dust during the Depression of the 1930s, it took some time to reclaim the farms. But the people returned to build dams to retain the runoff, to farm more in harmony with the cycles of nature, and to plant more trees to anchor the soil.

In at least one Heartland state the pioneers brought their trees with them. When the westward wagons crossed the eastern boundary of Nebraska at the Missouri River, in the early 1860s, the settlers, like the ones in the Dakota caravans, searched the horizon for trees. Very few were to be found. But 10 years later J. Sterling Morton, a Nebraska journalist who later served as U.S. Secretary of Agriculture, suggested that one day of the year be designated for planting trees. And so Arbor Day, now a national observance, began. In Nebraska alone, a million trees were subsequently planted, presaging the formation of the Nebraska National Forest. It was the first completely "man-made" forest in the nation.

Whether the forests are man-made or man-managed, they exist in every Heartland state. In southern Ohio, Indiana, Illinois, and Missouri, where the Wisconsin glacier did not reach, are timbered hills and clear lakes. For 400 miles along Ohio's southern border the Ohio River has attracted steel mills, power plants, and factories—most of them powered by coal. But clusters of willow, sycamore, and ash fall away from the river. There may even be an orchard now and then frequented by the ghost of Johnny Appleseed.

Indiana is flatly agricultural except at the extreme north

and south. Steel is produced in the north, but alongside the grimy mills are the Indiana Dunes, a wild panorama of shifting sands rising above the shores of Lake Michigan. Some of these dunes are desertlike, while others are covered with small trees and binder grass. In the south is scenic Brown County, where the autumn foliage of the hardwood forests attracts visitors from across the nation.

Illinois has its limestone bluffs, the Mississippi palisades, in the north and the Ozarks in the south. Missouri boasts the more famous Ozarks, and there Lake of the Ozarks and hundreds of other spring-fed lakes break up the rugged landscape.

In Minnesota, Wisconsin, and Michigan there are millions of acres of wilderness, plus thousands of lakes, to tempt vacationers and sportsmen. These states have some prairie vistas, too. Minnesota's pipestone country—red stone from which Indians made peace pipes—in the southwestern part of the state has prairie grass that looks as wild and unfettered as it did the first time white men saw it.

Forests cover about half of Wisconsin, and in the north central part there are higher elevations that look as rugged as they did before the glaciers came.

Michigan has such a natural, unspoiled countenance that more of it is used for recreation than for any other purpose. Iowa, the "biggest cornfield on earth," has an area in the northeast so rugged it is called Little Switzerland—a panoply of high buttes and cliffs jutting out along the rivers. The Indians also left their mark here in animal-shaped burial grounds.

Western Nebraska is more than corn country. Toadstool Park has huge rocks carved by erosion. Agate Fossil Beds National Monument is a place where fossils of extinct plains mammals are found. They are thought to go back about 20 million years.

What, then, is the Heartland? It is tractors growling across the broad fields. It is a robot welding an automobile frame. It is also children gathering Indian arrowheads in dozens of places where native Americans once ruled the territory. It is unearthing prehistoric skeletons, hiking in the wilderness, poking among the ashes of ancient volcanic formations, or stalking wild game with camera or gun. Reclaimed and preserved, much of the Heartland is as it was 150 or more years ago.

Grandfather cleared his homestead farm so that the corn and clover could grow, but he did not clear all of it. He left hundreds of trees standing, including 200 maple trees, to provide sap for his spring "run." Many farmers followed the same pattern. They preserved the woods, and thousands of those woods break the sameness of a landscape now engaged in growing food and fiber on a mass scale.

Today, one can still go from the prevailing openness of the tilled acres into the coolness and mystery of the woods. The woods are now, and have always been, a place for renewal. All things grow here in haphazard beauty instead of in the neat and ordered rows of the tilled land. There is a harmonizing of the tame and the wild in these woods and pastures: smooth and rounded slopes, jagged gullies, short

mowed meadows, and scruffy wild grass. The sunlight, so harsh on the cultivated rows, falls softened and gracious in the open spaces in the woods. The white oak and elm, the hickory and walnut trees cast their shadows in variegated patterns. There is likely to be clover humming with bees, wild gooseberry bushes, sassafras bushes, catnip, and elderberry blooming its creamy green-white tufts of lace.

Deeper in the woods, the wild flowers have given no ground for 150 years. I search them out every spring—the blue-purple windflowers, the Dutchman's breeches, the cowslips, the violets, and the saucy jacks-in-the-pulpit. The little stream turns east and leaves a northern bank shaded for the ferns breaking out of their leafy nests. Some of these flowers we shall transplant, duplicating the ritual of scores of grandparents who brought their house flowers from the woods.

This natural oasis is not much different from the time Grandfather saw it first. The tempo of living has quickened, but the cycle of seedtime and harvest continues with increasingly abundant yields from the "clearings" he made, confirming the judgment of those who chose this place over all the other places they could have gone.

Left– MUNISING FALLS, PICTURED ROCKS NATIONAL LAKESHORE / MICHIGAN

Above– ST. CROIX RIVER DALLES, INTERSTATE STATE PARK / MINNESOTA-WISCONSIN

Left– MAPLE AND BIRCH, VOYAGEURS NATIONAL PARK / MINNESOTA

Right– MINER'S CASTLE, LAKE SUPERIOR, PICTURED ROCKS NATIONAL LAKESHORE / MICHIGAN

Above– DUNE GRASS, INDIANA DUNES NATIONAL LAKESHORE / INDIANA

Right– SLUMP BLOCKS, OLD MAN'S CAVE AREA, HOCKING HILLS STATE PARK / OHIO

Overleaf– MISSOURI RIVER AT BISMARCK / NORTH DAKOTA

Above– CLAY FORMS ALONG MISSOURI RIVER NEAR HUFF / NORTH DAKOTA

Right– LITTLE MISSOURI RIVER COUNTRY, THEODORE ROOSEVELT NATIONAL PARK / NORTH DAKOTA

Left– MOONRISE, CHIMNEY ROCK NATIONAL HISTORIC SITE / NEBRASKA

Below– MOONRISE, MONUMENT ROCKS / KANSAS

GRANITES ALONG NORTH SHORE OF LAKE TAHOE / NEVADA

The High Country

Rooftop of the Continent

BY DAVID SUMNER

AMERICA'S HIGH COUNTRY IS AN ASTONISH-ingly vast and varied province. From Devils Tower in northeast Wyoming it reaches westward to the multiple, isolated, riblike ranges of Nevada. From the gracefully sculpted peaks of Montana's Glacier National Park, tight against the Canadian border, it plunges south to the desert tablelands of Monument Valley in southern Utah. From the depths of Idaho's rugged western edge in Hells Canyon it flows eastward in peak and plain to the waving wheat fields of Colorado's eastern third.

Backbone of this region is the great Rocky Mountain chain dropping south from Montana to southern Colorado and beyond, sprawling laterally from the Front Range to the height of mountains surrounding Lake Tahoe, a complexity of innumerable systems collectively known as the Rockies. But much of the High Country is not mountainous. More than half of Montana, much of Idaho, a third of Colorado, a quarter of Wyoming are plains. The Great Basin comprising most of Nevada and a lot of Utah has its mountain ranges, but much of it consists of irrigated valleys and flat, dry lake beds. This

unique self-contained area has no outlet to the sea but drains into the desert sands or into depressions like the Great Salt Lake. The Colorado Plateau is heavily cut by rivers of snow-melt water from distant mountains. Much of the region is desert: Nevada and Utah are our two driest states; western Colorado is largely desert; so is much of Wyoming, most of southern Idaho, and a good bit of Montana.

The misconception that the Rockies and their associated westerly ranges are all of a piece is dispelled only as one flies over them or travels through them by car or train. The Rocky Mountains are, in fact, a massive chain of ranges that in their total context run from Alaska to the southern tip of South America. Running along this erratic weaving line, frequently veering and looping laterally, is the Continental Divide, the crest of the Rockies that separates the waters that flow east from those that run west. Climb to the rim of the Divide in any of a dozen places by car, a hundred on horseback, a thousand on foot, and you can see how fine this line is.

In southwestern Colorado's San Juan range, for example, near the tiny 1880s silver camp of Lake City, the Divide traces

Colorado
Idaho
Montana
Nevada
Utah
Wyoming

a meandering line along a vast rolling expanse of grassy alpine tundra, the land above the trees. Spines of rock and sharp ridges that often characterize the Divide elsewhere are largely absent here. Instead, viewed from above, the terrain seems more like a high, gentle, undulating plain. Almost lost is a small, unnamed lake that seems to lie exactly on the crest of the Divide.

Look closely and you'll see that the land tilts just enough southward so this three-acre scenic lake drains gently into Pole Creek, then more swiftly into the upper Rio Grande, and ultimately into the Gulf of Mexico and to the Atlantic thousands of miles to the east. Look more closely and you'll see that a slight northward slant (a minor earthquake could do the job) would change everything: The same unnamed lake would drain down Cataract Creek into the Lake Fork of the Gunnison River, then into the main Gunnison, next into the mighty Colorado, and finally into the Gulf of California, an arm of the Pacific.

When I moved to this region from the East Coast in the 1960s, I was first bemused by the number of different ranges—

then agog, finally challenged: I wanted to hike and explore every one of them, but the more I studied maps, the more that became an obviously gargantuan task. Colorado, I learned, has 33 named ranges; Idaho has 81. Colorado alone has more than 50 peaks above 14,000 feet.

To date I've explored some 20 High Country ranges. The rest lure me on, their names like the folk poetry of the West: Tobacco Root and Bitterroot; Wasatch and Sawatch; White River, Wind River, and Lost River; Absaroka and Cochetopa; Elkhead, Rabbit Ears, Mosquito, and Swan. And over in Nevada is an irregular, disjunct array of ranges that few Americans have ever heard of: the Goshute and Pequop mountains; the Toana, Reveille, and Pancake ranges; the Toiyabe, and many more.

All are inviting, each has its own distinct way. One of these days I'm going to hike Montana's Crazy Mountains simply because of the name. After you have lived in and roamed America's High Country for a spell, the differences become increasingly vivid. In Colorado I go to the San Juans for an experience in sheer mass; to the Sangre de Cristos for

Overleaf– SNAKE RIVER, GRAND TETON NATIONAL PARK / WYOMING

intense, angular power; to the Elks for a finer, sculptured grace. Each range, like a favorite national park, has its distinctions.

You soon learn what areas have their special gifts: Wyoming's Wind River range has an awesome mix of high lakes, small glaciers, and granite walls; the Tarryall Mountains in Colorado have more bizarre granites, shaped like gargoyles and ghosts, but relatively little water; the Beaverhead Mountains, along the Montana-Idaho border, are unique for their history—especially Lemhi Pass, where the explorers Lewis and Clark first crossed the Continental Divide on their epic journey to the Pacific in 1805.

Travel down the twisted dirt road on the west flank of this pass and you will find a commemorative marker with a quotation from the Lewis and Clark journal: "Here we first tasted the waters of the mighty Columbia River." Shoshone Indians who lived in the area had told them that they were in the Pacific watershed, and the explorers were soon eating salmon they obtained in trade with the Indians, further proof that these waters drained to the Pacific.

All of this region was Indian country—as was all of America at one time—the land of the Shoshone and Blackfoot, the Arapaho and Cheyenne, the Ute and Paiute, the Nez Perce and Assiniboine, the Lakota and Crow. Some tribes had been pushed into the region by settlers on the plains to the east. Before long these native peoples would experience more pressure from the growing populations of the white man.

The first of these were the mountain men—John Colter, a member of the Corps of Discovery under Lewis and Clark who elected to stay in the northern Rockies; Jim Bridger, Ceran St. Vrain, Jedediah Smith. Smith, whose scholarly biography is subtitled "The Opening of the West," was with the first party to cross South Pass, which became the standard route over the Divide, the route of the Oregon Trail. He was the first to discover the Great Basin, to realize it had no outlet, to travel its length and breadth. He knew this High Country from the Missouri River to the Green, from the Great Salt Lake to the Flathead country.

Following the paths pioneered by these "white Indians"—who trapped beaver, often took Indian wives, and learned the lay of the land—the settlers came, flowing through the region like rivers along narrowly prescribed routes to the fertile, well-watered valleys farther west and to the coastal lowlands. It is a curious fact that this Rocky Mountain region was settled only after the West Coast was well populated, when the tide of immigration swept back from the Pacific into the High Country.

It was the Mormons, a tough and determined people full of religious zeal, who first subdued this region. Driven out of the East and the Midwest for their religious beliefs and practices, the Latter-day Saints settled in the valley of the Great Salt Lake, then colonized what later became Idaho, Wyoming, Montana, Colorado, Nevada, and well beyond, where their beliefs remain the single most influential religious force.

In this Mormon land lie two ranges notably isolated from their neighbors—like the Mormons in the early days. The Henry Mountains, the last major range discovered in the

YUCCA, CHOLLA, AND JOSHUA TREE IN
RED ROCK CANYON / NEVADA

United States and home to a small herd of free-ranging bison, tower over the canyonlands of southeastern Utah. In Utah's great west desert where the Pony Express route goes into Nevada, the Deep Creek Mountains rise to 12,000 feet from the dry bed of an ancient lake, a range so isolated in elevation and distance that unique species of plants, fish, and insects have evolved here. From the summit of this range you can see—on a clear day—almost the whole Great Basin. One characteristic of the region is open space, broad vistas, a sense of vastness.

The high valleys and tablelands are themselves a surprise. Of all the sights in Colorado, none is more purely breathtaking than the drive southwest from Denver on U.S. 285 over Kenosha Pass to South Park. In the High Country "park" means large, open, high-mountain valley (as "hole" signifies smaller, narrower, mountain-rimmed valley). South Park is huge—100 by 50 miles of windswept grassland erratically broken by low, rounded ridges thatched with fir, spruce, limber pine, and—less often—aspen. This is lush, green cattle country in summer, but a bitter no-man's-land in winter, especially when ground blizzards whip across the park, reducing visibility to a foot or two. Ground blizzards occur when severe low-elevation winds blast loose snow from the already-fallen pack, whipping it relentlessly across the land. Stand in one of these phenomena (you'll have to lean hard into the wind) and you may be able to see the stars overhead but not your own feet planted in the drifting snow.

Rivers carve great canyons from the mountains too, not only the famous ones like the Grand Canyon of the Yellowstone, the Black Canyon of the Gunnison, and the legendary Hells Canyon of the Snake, but also countless other mountain gorges whose names only begin to suggest their variety: Bluejay, Dark, Crystal, Canyon del Diablo, Forest, Impassable, and literally hundreds more including the popular rafting runs on the Salmon, Yampa, Green, Dolores, Arkansas, Selway, and Flathead rivers.

The truly remarkable canyon country of this region lies out of the mountains, around the edges—as if the forces of geology had found a need to match the grandeur of the peaks with another kind of majesty below. East of the southern Colorado Rockies, Purgatory Canyon (called by natives "Picket Wire" and sometimes "Piggitwa") cuts a sinuous gash into the high plains. In southwest Idaho the great Bruneau Canyon, a wild river at its bottom and more than enough rattlesnakes for a roundup, appears as a sudden, inexplicable crack in the land.

For the fullest canyon feast, explore south of the Uinta Range in Utah and west of Colorado's sprawling San Juans. Southern Utah's remarkable canyon country is the site of America's greatest concentration of national parks: Arches, Bryce, Canyonlands, Capitol Reef, and Zion. All of them are carved, one way or another, by waters that gather from mountain snowfields at higher elevations—snowfields that, each spring, send fresh water, filled with sand and silt, to carve canyon floors deeper and bends wider, more undercut and overhanging. These same spring waters, when they reach Utah's canyon country, also sharpen spires and pinnacles, widen natural arches, and begin their work of creating new

Left– LOWER FALLS OF THE YELLOWSTONE, YELLOWSTONE NATIONAL PARK / WYOMING

Below– DOUGLAS FIR, LIVINGSTONE RANGE, GLACIER NATIONAL PARK / MONTANA

AUTUMN TRANSITION, ANIMAS RIVER CANYON, NEEDLES RANGE / COLORADO

rock forms wherever the geology is suitable. Utah has one area called Goblin Valley, full of red rocks carved into strange forms. The town of Mexican Hat is named for a sombrero-like rock formation nearby. Once, hiking in an isolated patch of Canyonlands National Park, I came upon a perfect mushroom-shaped rock twice my height. Out here you learn to expect the unexpected.

Many of the canyons of this area—geologically known as the Colorado Plateau—are large, carved by great rivers. The Green River carves Desolation and Gray canyons, Labyrinth and Stillwater, and the Colorado carves rapids-strewn Cataract Canyon. One stretch of Labyrinth Canyon is so convoluted that the river flows 28 miles to gain nine miles in a direct line.

But for a canyon to explore and enjoy on a temperate spring day, my choice is a 30-square-mile infinitely tangled system in the western reach of Canyonlands National Park called the Maze. It is remote: You must hike 13 miles overland just to get your first look at it. "A labyrinth with the roof removed," it has been called, but that barely begins to describe what must be the most intensely concentrated canyon system in the world.

Standing on the rim facing the Maze, you are confronted with a 250-degree panorama of canyons—winding, twisting, sinuous—that resemble nothing so much as the infinite, intricate folds of a human brain. But descend the 1,200 feet from rim to canyon floor—using toe holds, friction, and, if you are carrying a heavy pack, a rope—and you arrive in a wholly different world. You lose your bird's-eye perspective and find yourself in that maze, faced with a lifetime of choices of high desert canyons to explore, an experience both frightening and exciting. The red and white strata of candy-striped walls offer no clue to the way out of the labyrinth, and you proceed like the first person on earth.

Rocky summit and deep valley, graceful ridge and twisted canyon floor. All this is America's High Country to explore. Major John Wesley Powell explored it in 1869, leading a small expedition through the canyons of the Green and Colorado rivers in Wyoming, Colorado, Utah, and beyond. Powell fathered both the U.S. Geologic Survey and the Bureau of Reclamation. He dreamed of turning this arid region into productive land so that it could be settled. He set in motion a century-long movement to correct nature's mistake in leaving so large a region arid.

For an overriding characteristic of this region is its lack of water, a major reason so few people settled here—along with the fact that winters are long and severe and growing seasons correspondingly short and fickle. Even today this six-state region is sparsely populated, with not quite 8 million people in its 629,000 square miles—that's an average of fewer than 13 people per square mile.

The area may not seem all that dry. Many of the nation's best-known ski resorts are here—Alta, Aspen, Big Sky, Jackson Hole, Snowbird, Sun Valley, Vail—and they measure snowfall in feet, not inches. There's a lot of moisture stored in the snowpack, but the moisture comes at the wrong time for crops. The moisture that falls here can't be utilized except for winter sports, and it all runs off somewhere else. The major cities of the region—Denver, Salt Lake City, Boise, Las Vegas, Great Falls, Casper—all anticipate water shortages in the next decade; some experience them already.

This region is rich in national parks and monuments, wildlife refuges and recreation areas, forests and national resource lands. In fact, the federal government manages more than half of this land. It has vast mineral wealth and energy resources: gold, silver, copper, molybdenum, lead, and zinc; oil, gas, uranium, coal, tar sands, oil shale, and solar energy—and all these competing uses demand water. The pinto bean, sugar beet, and alfalfa field are all grown on irrigated land, but irrigation pumping requires vast amounts of electricity: Use the water for irrigation, and there may not be enough to produce the electricity to pump that water. In this land of the fly fisherman and the logger, the elk hunter and the energy developer, the wilderness backpacker and the hard-rock miner—who may be the same individuals—there simply isn't enough water to go around.

From my home at an elevation of 8,885 feet in the Colorado Rockies, higher than any point east of the Mississippi, the first snows of the season may be visible on the high peaks as early as Labor Day. One year the summits picked up a dusting on August 4: The high strata looked like layers of frosting on a cake. Another year, on July 23, I hiked to a favorite spot not far from where I live, the scenic Oh-Be-Joyful Valley. There, at timberline and above, I found snowfields from the previous winter. In a high lake, large chunks of ice floated like pieces of an old glacier, and on the adjoining slope I could have skied.

My home is in a small mountain community, Crested Butte (pop. 1,200), which in many ways typifies this region.

Like many other towns, it was born in the 1880s, a supply center for the hurley-burley, boom-or-bust silver mines higher in the mountains. For several decades it was a coal town; for the last two, it has been an attractive out-of-the-way ski resort. I am lucky: Crested Butte is the kind of place where many Americans dream of living, a mountain Brigadoon.

As I write, it is high autumn, the first week in October. Outside my studio window brisk winds are gusting from the west: Light snow flurries churn in the bright sunlight. In the front yard, leaves of the elaborate, many-branched cottonwoods have yellowed and turned gold. Just outside the town limits on the north-facing flank of Gibson's Ridge, scattered patches of aspen are an even brighter yellow. If I drive the gravel road 10 miles west and south to Ohio Pass, I will find that the aspens have taken over completely, flowing down whole mountainsides in bright avalanches of shimmering gold. This is truly fall in the High Country.

From fall in Crested Butte, turn to midwinter in Wyoming's Yellowstone National Park, not the storied part with all the geysers and falls, but rather the remote southwest corner where the Bechler River oxbows through broad meadows. In February the landscape is leveled by many feet of snow, ideal terrain for ski touring. In the week I spend here—traveling 65 miles, camping in the snow—the winter weather has a rhythm, though in the High Country you can never count on it: three days of bright sun and luminous, starry nights with temperatures near zero, then a warmer day with snow followed by three more days of sun, and then another of snow. It could be colder, but I am lucky.

Yellowstone makes up for the seasonal chill in its offerings. When the first fur trappers probed the area in 1811, they were intrigued by the thermal phenomena. But when they

Left– WINTER SUNRISE ON CATHEDRAL GROUP, GRAND TETON NATIONAL PARK / WYOMING

Above– PIKES PEAK AND GARDEN OF THE GODS / COLORADO

returned to civilization with tales of their strange encounters, of mud volcanoes, geysers, hot springs, and grumbling fumaroles, their words were dismissed as fiction. Not until the early 1870s, when photographer William Henry Jackson—hauling a huge, cumbersome camera, wet photographic plates (glass), and all his chemicals on a mule named Hypo—made the first real images of Yellowstone's wonders, would the rest of America believe. His works, displayed in the Capitol rotunda in Washington, D.C., helped convince Congress to designate Yellowstone as the country's (and the world's) first national park.

From the rich yellows of autumn, the color of the land is reduced to black and white and drab conifer tones. But what winter takes away in color, it gives back in design: Tiny tracks crisscross and meander over the snow, telling wonderful and terrible tales; wind-sculptured snow and rimed trees, ghosts in the steamy air, stimulate the imagination; the icy edge of an open river is fine lace.

Even as the snow grows deeper with each winter storm, the days grow longer with the promise of spring in the aspen and willow buds. As the snow recedes, wild flowers edge upward from the desert and prairie to the foothills and lower slopes, returning color to the land. The warblers return and the insect hatches on the rivers herald another fishing season. Rising runoff waters mark the beginning of whitewater season. Spring may be the region's most fickle season for fair weather, but it's the best for river running.

At 7,000 feet in Idaho's Sawtooth range on my drive to the Middle Fork of the Salmon, drifts of snow still lie on the pass and a brief snowstorm flurries in mid-June. Creeks are swollen and meadows are swampy with standing water. At the launch site, the Middle Fork surges near flood, still clear but swift and loud, crashing over rocks, foaming through a narrow gorge.

The Middle Fork is one of the Rockies' most exciting rivers, by most standards too big to be called a "fork" of anything. It flows for more than 100 miles, dropping 3,000 feet through a granitic canyon, the walls of which rise—brooding and gray—4,000 feet above the frigid water. The Middle Fork, one of the original wild rivers in a national system of wild

Left– SNAKE RIVER, BIRDS OF PREY NATURAL AREA / IDAHO

Below– JUDITH RIVER, MISSOURI RIVER TRIBUTARY / MONTANA

and scenic rivers, has, by guidebook count, 341 rapids in its lower runable 96 miles, many of them mere riffles. But it is river enough to keep one on a keen edge, and during spring runoff, it adds a note of fear.

The current literally yanks my boat downriver, the surge of its water and the energy of the season becoming one. The maneuvering to avoid rocks and churning holes, icy waves and nasty snags is exhilarating, tiring. The river is fast, the water cold, but I have less trouble with the river than with the weather, which again has a pattern: rain every day. Twice it snows, but that is spring on the Middle Fork. By the time my party reaches the main Salmon—near the point at which Lewis and Clark turned away from the raging river to cross the mountains on horseback—summer is here, both by the calendar and by the weather, which improves as we float out of Impassable Canyon.

Spring weather is iffy, and autumn can bring sudden snowstorms to spoil a trip, even threaten life. Fear of winter's avalanches and extreme temperatures may keep me out of my favorite places much of the year, but summer is the time for backpacking in the mountains. On the drive home from the Middle Fork—through the desert, past the canyonlands, into the mountains—I plan my next trip into the vastness of America's High Country where summer reaches its climax: My choice this time is the Maroon Bells-Snowmass Wilderness not far from home.

The name comes from three mountains: the two Maroon Bells, which are shaped and colored as they are named, and Snowmass, so called for a perennial snowfield on its eastern flank. This wilderness lies halfway between Crested Butte and the resort town of Aspen. From either, it's a short drive and a shorter hike to the wilderness boundary.

Backpacking is a quieter, more personal activity than either river running or cross-country skiing. I hike north from Crested Butte into a large bowl called Scofield Basin, then over a ridge and a pass into another bowl, Farvert Basin, which rolls in a modified stairstep to the southern flank of South Maroon Bell. If autumn is yellow and winter is white, summer in the High Country is green, an almost iridescent rainbow green that immediately strikes the eye. Yet that green is deceiving because on closer inspection it is seen to be dotted with innumerable vivid wild flowers.

I am talking about the zone known as alpine tundra, where life is so severe the plants have adopted an array of defenses against the wind and cold, short growing season, and deep-snow pressure. They are largely perennials, requiring more than a year or two to mature in the harsh setting. Most of them are smaller, tougher, brighter in color than their lowland relatives. They may grow in dense clusters for insulation or have soft gray hairs to protect them from the ultraviolet light in this land of thin air and little atmospheric screening.

I hike here with full pack and marveling eyes, stopping to admire, photograph, and absorb. Any day now the first storm will again dust the higher peaks with snow. This gentle tundra, soft and rolling, will turn colorful with autumn as the seasons flow into one another in a recurring pattern that is as consistent as the hydrologic cycle. Water falls into this High Country to be stored as snow and ice, to be held by shady slopes and protective vegetation, to be captured by plants, and to be carried away to distant oceans where it forms clouds again, eventually to be returned by the winds to the skies over the High Country.

Sometimes the seasons get mixed up or overlap one another: It snows in midsummer or a sunny warm spell brings an unseasonable thaw to January. Sometimes the water cycle goes haywire and floods the valleys, or a drought makes the arid region even drier for a year or two. But in the long run there is a constancy in these natural systems you can depend on, even as we have come to depend on systems we have created—political systems and social systems—to preserve our natural world in bits and pieces here and there as wilderness areas, wild and scenic rivers, parks and monuments.

The national park idea, first implemented with the creation of Yellowstone in 1872, has expanded to include a nationwide network of parks, monuments, historic sites, and recreation areas. It was the first step in a long progression of conservation measures that have left a bolder imprint on the High Country than on any other region of the United States south of Alaska. In more recent years we have created a national wilderness preservation system (1964) and a national wild and scenic rivers system (1968).

The wilderness areas are phenomena primarily of the national forests, though the National Park System and the Bureau of Land Management have also created a network of preserves embracing lands that have outstanding primeval qualities, to remind people of what this country was like before man first set foot on it.

In a sense the wilderness system is a bank where the principal is saved, earns interest, and is available to use if it is ever needed desperately enough. It is protected from short-term economic exploitation for the people of the nation to use as they see fit: for scientific study and public recreation, for genetic and species diversification and wildlife habitat, for watershed protection and livestock grazing.

Lands designated as wilderness basically cannot be destroyed or even encroached upon by mechanical devices. There are no roads. Logging is prohibited and mining carefully regulated. Access is limited. The Wilderness Act of 1964 has both historic and ecologic significance in that it attempts to preserve natural systems in a way that will provide scientists with information on their functioning without human disturbance, while it gives lay people a chance—in a remnant but very forceful form—to experience the wilderness that once covered the continent.

The experience of travel into a wilderness area today is akin to that of the country's first pioneers. A few of the dangers and uncertainties have been removed, but you can still know a sense of wonder, feel fear, find solitude, experience what self-reliance really means. You may encounter a grizzly bear, get lost, or even freeze to death if you aren't prepared—it happens every year in America's High Country. If wilderness means anything, such possibilities must exist. Yet the farther you have to travel on your own, the more rewarding the experience. In wilderness you have to earn your way, whether on foot or on horseback, on touring ski

ABOVE LOGAN PASS, CONTINENTAL DIVIDE EAST, GLACIER NATIONAL PARK / MONTANA

Left– QUEENS GARDEN, BRYCE CANYON NATIONAL PARK / UTAH

Below– ERODED TOWER IN LIGHT BLIZZARD, CATHEDRAL GORGE / NEVADA

or snowshoe—or in a muscle-powered boat on a wild river.

You can appreciate the High Country from an airplane flying over the Rockies, looking down on the vast landscape highlighted by forest and snowfield, marked by irrigated valley and manmade reservoir. You can see it by car or train, but to experience it you have to become part of it. It can be as low as the bedrock of the Snake River in Hells Canyon or as high as the windswept bristlecone pines atop Nevada's Wheeler Peak; as level as Bonneville Salt Flats or as rough and rugged as the Waterpocket Fold. It can be as dry as a black widow's web in the hollow of a juniper log or as wet as a beaver's belly; as hot as a barren blackrock desert or as cold as the chill factor at the top of the Jackson Hole Ski Area tram in an 80-mile-an-hour winter wind.

It may be winter-white, summer-green, autumn-yellow, or as multicolored as the algae in a Yellowstone hot pool or the rock formations in Utah's Kodachrome Basin. It is vast and varied, a collection of states and a state of mind that is no more bound by state lines than the rivers it nurtures. The High Country has a character all its own, a hang-loose, homespun, friendly western attitude that is part of the American character. It is a land that has shaped its people, a harsh land and a beautiful one.

Even as the land has shaped its people, so the people have shaped the land. They have dammed its rivers, gouged its mountains, and clearcut its forests. But they have also made the desert bloom in unlikely spots and preserved its special places, its unique features, and its character.

Left– COLUMBINES IN SAN JUAN MOUNTAINS / COLORADO

Right– COLUMBINES IN GRANITE, MOSQUITO RANGE / COLORADO

Above– ICEBERG LAKE AND MOUNT HENKEL,
GLACIER NATIONAL PARK / MONTANA

Left– ALPINE POOL, ISLAND LAKE TRAIL, BRIDGER WILDERNESS,
WIND RIVER RANGE / WYOMING

Above– AUTUMN STORM OVER STILLWATER FORK,
BEAR RIVER, UINTA RANGE / UTAH

Left– PAHOEHOE LAVA, CRATERS OF THE MOON NATIONAL MONUMENT / IDAHO

Above– STEAMING TERRACE, MAMMOTH HOT SPRINGS, YELLOWSTONE NATIONAL PARK / WYOMING

Left– GREAT GOOSENECKS, SAN JUAN RIVER / UTAH

Above– RAINBOW BRIDGE NATIONAL MONUMENT / UTAH

WHITE SANDS NATIONAL MONUMENT / NEW MEXICO

The Southwest

A Land of Infinite Variety

BY TONY HILLERMAN

THE THREE OF US—MARIE, THE BLUE HERON, and I—are all Southwesterners. On this balmy January day, we are in Texas, Marie and I watching birds near Washington Beach, where the Rio Grande joins the Gulf of Mexico, and the Blue Heron 30 yards away, shuffling along in the shallows stirring up a meal. A week ago we three were doing approximately the same things 800 miles upstream in New Mexico's Bosque del Apache Wildlife Refuge—my wife and I admiring the snow geese on the open water of the marshes, while the Blue Heron stalked along shin deep among the cattails, long beak poised and beady eyes alert.

Same river, same Blue Heron (Marie says no, last week's heron was older and female), same Southwest. But all else is different. Take winter. Winter at the Gulf Coast end of the Rio Grande is palm trees, shirtsleeves, and a balmy south breeze blowing up from the Yucatan tropics. But last week winter in New Mexico was a light icing of snow on the Coyote Hills, a bit of frost on the earlobes, and the dark blue sky of high country aridity. In the high country of New Mexico

and Arizona, winter can be 40 below zero and 100 inches of snow. Here on the fertile flatlands of the Texas Gulf, winter seems an implausible rumor from another world.

In Oklahoma and Texas, spring is the time that inspired the poets. It comes early, exploding northward from the Gulf with the spreading colors of bluebonnets, poppies, spring beauties, wild violets—more wild flowers than I can name. The pastures turn blue and white and the creeks smell of plum blossoms. But in New Mexico and Arizona there are two springs. Below 6,000 feet, spring is 18 days of blowing dirt followed by summer, while in the mountains, spring climbs slowly up from the foothills. In the highest country, in the meadows between the spruce forests, it doesn't arrive until July and lingers into August, with columbines, wild irises, and lupines blooming everywhere.

Summer is just as different. While Texas and Oklahoma are smothering in August humidity, the dry June forest fire season is already over farther west. August brings what the Navajo calls "time when thunder is awake"—monsoon season. Towering thunderheads build over the mountains each

Arizona
New Mexico
Oklahoma
Texas

afternoon and cool the valleys with showers.

In the desert, this late summer rainy season substitutes for spring. Yuccas send forth their towering spikes of blossoms, and sand poppies and asters flourish everywhere. Even the Sonoran and Yuma deserts, dry as they are, are ablaze with sand verbena, prickly poppy, and the rich, red blossoms of hedgehog cactus.

Autumn in Texas and Oklahoma is red and orange with the turning leaves of hardwoods. Autumn in New Mexico and Arizona has no reds. Just the gold of cottonwoods along the rivers, bright yellow aspen and chamisa in the higher country, and the silver of sage and seeding desert grasses.

That marked degree of difference is the story of the Southwest. No other region of the United States matches its wild leap across the spectrum of zones of climate, biology, and geology. Our Blue Heron, for example, has already changed his environment dramatically by flying down the Rio Grande from the desert landscape of central New Mexico to Texas's western tip. He can change it again by simply flying up the long curve of Texas coastline. As he moves

northeast along Laguna Madre, over Padre Island, and across Galveston Bay, the shoreline beneath him begins to change. The great white sweep of sand, the high dunes, the blowing grasses fade away. He flies into more humid territory, into the wetter winds and cloudier skies of bayou country at the mouth of the Sabine River. Here no sharp division of blue water and white beach draws a line between continent and ocean. This eastern margin of Texas is a drowned land of salt marshes, tidal pools, great expanses of floating hyacinth, sheets of water coated pale green with acres of blooming chickweed—a place where universes of triangle grass are being gobbled down by hundreds of thousands of voracious waterfowl spending their winter vacation. No great, sandy barrier islands here. The coastline changes with the tides.

Why this marked difference along the same coastline? Here the winds make the difference. The sky over the Sabine River is not the sky over the Rio Grande. There winter winds blow from the north—drier and cooler. Here on the Sabine the Gulf winds dominate. Average sunshine decreases. Average humidity soars. Rainfall almost doubles. In the same

Overleaf– SUNRISE, MONUMENT VALLEY NAVAJO TRIBAL PARK / ARIZONA

Above– RIO GRANDE RIVER AND SIERRA DEL CARMEN, BIG BEND NATIONAL PARK / TEXAS

year the south coast may receive less than 30 inches of rain while more than 60 inches drench the Sabine wetlands. The winds determine the landscape here. But as you move west, it becomes a matter of altitude.

The Southwest is tilted. It slopes out of the warm Gulf waters with almost incredible gradualness, rising toward the north and west. Dallas, the glitterdome of north Texas, is some 300 miles inland from the mouth of Galveston Bay, but the land has risen less than 500 feet—less than the height of a modest downtown office building. Follow the Rio Grande 200 miles upstream to Laredo and you have risen only 440 feet above the sea. Tulsa, in the northeastern corner of the Southwest, is more than 500 miles from salt water but only 600 feet above the tideline. As you move westward from the Gulf marshes, from the green rivers of eastern Oklahoma, the land rises steadily. The rolling croplands of central Texas and Oklahoma lie 1,000 feet above sea level, the wheat and cattle country of the panhandles is 2,000 feet and higher, rising faster as the New Mexico border is crossed, then soaring into the ridges of the Southern Rockies. In the 1,300 miles from Port Arthur, Texas, to Yuma, Arizona, you move from a low, flat, humid landscape into high, dry, vertical country where nothing much is flat except the table-top mesas and the bottoms of intermountain valleys.

Some years ago this "tilt" was inadvertently—and fatally—demonstrated by a private pilot with the help of a shaker of martinis. He left Hobby International Airport in Houston en route to San Diego via Albuquerque, climbed to 5,000 feet, set his autopilot for that altitude, and headed west, tapping the martinis en route. Apparently he was fast asleep later that day when a rancher saw his Cessna, still cruising faithfully at 5,000 feet above sea level but now less than three feet above the ground, fly through a barbed-wire fence and into a hayfield in eastern New Mexico's Guadalupe County.

The Southwest is like two different worlds, and the Rio Grande, which ties these two together, illustrates that point. It seems like two rivers. The Spanish explorers who found its Texas end called it River of Palms or River of May and wrote reports praising it as a gentle, hospitable stream. But the Spanish who discovered it at what is now the New Mexico border, where it drowned their horses with sudden floods and then went completely dry, called it Rio Bravo del Norte, the Wild River of the North. Today the clear, icy snowmelt stream that boils over the black basalt boulders in the Taos Gorge—drawing daredevil rapids runners from across the world and killing them often enough to keep its reputation— is a different river than the stream that meanders through the cabbage fields of south Texas.

The Southwest needs east Texas as a contrast, for it is what the rest of the territory is not. It is lush, shady, damp, fecund, bursting with life—insect, plant, bird, bacterial, reptile, and mammal. Twelve million acres of pine, cypress, walnut, oak, magnolia, dogwood and, quite literally, a hundred other tree varieties are its dominant feature. The Big Thicket— once a bona fide wilderness—is here. Where road and terrain permit, much of this great forest has been cut over by loggers. The hardwoods and magnolias are mostly gone, and

Left– CANYON DEL MUERTO, CANYON DE CHELLY NATIONAL MONUMENT / ARIZONA

Below– NAVAJO HOME, YEI BE CHEI ROCKS, AND ROOSTER ROCK, MONUMENT VALLEY NAVAJO TRIBAL PARK / ARIZONA-UTAH

the pines are harvested like hay and replanted in orderly rows. The country also bears the scars of more than 25,000 oil wells, which have pumped an ocean of petroleum from under the forests. Since the famous Spindletop boom in 1901, east Texas oil production would be worth more than $100 billion at 1982 prices. The process has left in its wake pollution and creeks ruined by salt water. Cattlemen have added their brand, draining wetlands to make way for the grass this rich, black land will grow. Still, thousands of acres are left in the Big Thicket National Preserve and in scattered places where nature defends itself with swamps too boggy for exploitation.

The eastern fringe of Oklahoma is distinctly different. Here the Ouachita Mountains (pronounced Washita) and the Ozark Plateau intrude their pine-covered slopes into the valleys of the Arkansas, Red, and Little rivers. This is Oklahoma's hillbilly territory. Rainy country still, but the Gulf winds that drench the coastal swamps curl to the east and have lost much of their moisture this far north. This is steeply rolling land shaded by a mixture of soft pine and scores of deciduous species. It is poor country for grubbing out a living, but great for white-tailed deer, raccoons, and big mouth bass.

In fact, all of eastern and much of central Oklahoma is fishing country—a land of lakes produced in an orgy of dam building by the U.S. Army Corps of Engineers. There are the Grand, Gibson, Oologah, Pine Creek, Tenkiller, and Atoka reservoirs, Lake of the Cherokees, Eufaula, Murray, Texoma, Kaw, Keystone, Arbuckle, Canton, and numerous others.

When I was a boy in Oklahoma, one rowed along the shorelines of these reservoirs amid forests of drowned trees and sometimes over the chimneys of submerged creekside cabins. Time and decay have eliminated such obstacles now, leaving these lakes sheets of blue water abuzz with the outboard motors of bass fishermen and their mortal enemies, the water-skiers.

In Texas, the pine flats of the bayou country give way to open hill croplands, which transmute into the vast central flatness called the Grand Prairie. In Oklahoma the wooded hills are replaced by gently rolling grasslands—the Osage Hills, the Cherokee and Enid plains. This is family farm country, marked off in square miles by "section line" roads with a farmhouse about every half mile. It is a country where gullies left by exploitive cotton farming of 50 years ago are

now being healed by grass, time, and modern agricultural techniques. This is the territory that produced the "Okies" of John Steinbeck's *Grapes of Wrath.* The migration caused then by drought, Dust Bowl, and Depression has continued ever since on a slower scale, caused now by the high price of tractors and the low price of corn. Economics has meant bigger farms and fewer farmers, and the countryside is dotted with artifacts of that evolution—the abandoned, weatherbeaten, windowless shacks and collapsing barns left behind by those who sold out and moved to town.

This part of Oklahoma was the Southwest of my childhood, a place where the woods filled with fireflies on summer evenings, whippoorwills called from the hills, mockingbirds sang on moonlight nights. The gullies that killed the cornfields were mines for the red clay we used to mold

BLUEBONNETS AND INDIAN PAINTBRUSH, HILL COUNTRY / TEXAS

the "bullets" for our endless game of Cowboys and Indians. (Most of my playmates were genuine Indians—Pottawatomies, Seminoles, and Blackfeet—but their people had left the old gods behind when the government moved them to the Oklahoma Territory. Their sons, having learned who wins and who loses from the movies, insisted on taking their turn at the cowboy role.) It was also a place where—in contrast to New Mexico and Arizona—the humid air carried a cornucopia of smells: clover, dogwood blossoms, dust, the rotten-egg aroma of a distant oil well, the mustiness of old hay, plowed earth, horse urine, the spoiling windfalls under the apple tree, honeysuckle. Persons raised in the mountains, where the thin, dry air is a poor conductor of such perfumes, may spend their entire lives without learning how important the nose can be in stimulating nostalgia.

Here in central Oklahoma, and southward in Texas, you have moved across that vague boundary between what climatologists call the moist subhumid and the dry subhumid. In practical terms, you are in country where—in July and August—farmers pray for rain. In Texas as you move west from Austin you climb the vast Edwards Plateau and enter the beautiful Hill Country, where clear streams run through a land of folded, faulted limestone hills—a land of small fields, fenced feedlots, and pastures. It is mild, hospitable country, shaded and rolling, undramatic, but in the minds of many, the prettiest part of Texas. North, across the Red River Valley in Oklahoma, that state, too, puts on its most handsome face. In the Arbuckle Mountains, the structures left by ancient volcanic action mix with great folds of upthrust hills to form a landscape of ridges and narrow valleys. Again

there are limestone, clear streams, gushing springs, and places where underground heat produces geysers and fills the air with the smell of sulphur. To the west, the Wichita Mountains form a larger, more open setting. The world's largest buffalo herd roams the Wichita Mountains Wildlife Refuge, in a natural environment of prairie grasses and uncut timber—the way it was when the Kiowas, who have their reservation here, were "Lords of the Plains."

From the granite ridges of the Wichitas one looks westward toward those Great Plains. If one had to draw a line indicating where the "west" of the Southwest begins, the 100th meridian would be as fair a border as any. Before the white man came and exercised his power to change ecology, east of the 100th could have been described as a world dominated by trees, while the land west of that line was a world of grass. As you approach Oklahoma's western boundary, trees are already becoming scarcer—limited mostly to shading the creeks, which themselves have become less frequent as countryside dries and flattens. Grass is the dominant natural flora here, commonly a short bluestem giving way to needlegrass where fertility is low. The color, too, has changed. Grass here is a paler green, verging into the gray, tan, and silver of dry country species—grama, buffalo, Indian rice, and various bunch grasses. Except for irrigated fields and the cottonwood bosques of river valleys, you leave dark green behind you on the prairie.

In the Oklahoma Panhandle and north of Amarillo, Texas, this prairie country is called the High Plains. Southward, it's the Staked Plains, the Llano Estacado. Whatever the name, it is a treeless, undulating sea of grass. The Gulf winds rarely bring their moisture here—just enough in the High Plains to grow winter wheat. The landscape tends to overwhelm the eye with the single-season color of the grain: deep green in spring, gray-green with summer, merging into tan, then to harvest gold, the yellow-gray of stubblefields and, as winter looms, the rich black of the plowed and planted earth.

Farther south in Texas, diminishing rainfall makes wheat a bad gamble. These Staked Plains are watered by pumps tapping the Ogallala Aquifer, an underground lake that extends into New Mexico and as far north as Nebraska. But here the lake is running dry, the water table is falling too low for economic pumping, and the green summers of the Staked Plains are turning brown. Crops requiring less water are being developed, but it now seems likely that this part of the Southwest will eventually revert to something closer to its natural state, which was mesquite, dry country grasses, juniper, and cactus. My mother, who homesteaded in the Panhandle before pump irrigation, enriched my childhood with legends of the prairie's inhospitality to humankind. Hers were stories of sod dugout hardships, of hauling water, of dried cow chips burned for cooking fuel, of riding 20 miles just to see a tree, of blizzards blowing snow horizontally across the flatness, and of blistering summers where the only shade for miles around was under your own sunbonnet.

Goodbye to Greer County, where the blizzards arise,
Where the sun never rests, and the flea never dies,
And the wind never ceases, but always remains
Till it starves us to death on our government claim.

There were a hundred verses contained in that sodbuster ballad, each of them an ironic celebration of the Panhandle's intolerance of man.

Wherever you leave the prairie headed west, you go uphill, and uphill fast. The rise from the flatness of the Gulf has been slow for 700 miles. Now the climb is neither slow nor gradual. In eastern New Mexico you leave the Great Plains behind you. The horizon no longer fades into the distance. Now it is outlined by the blue shape of mountains.

Mountains are the dominant feature of New Mexico. Except for the eastern fringe, no part of the state is without them. The good maps name 73 ranges, from Animas to Zuni. They include seven peaks rising above 13,000 feet, 85 more than two miles high, and more than 300 notable enough to warrant names. All are part of the Southern Rockies and, with a few purely volcanic exceptions, they are arranged in irregular north-south ridges that feature an exhausted old volcano or two and that dominate the valleys their snow-packs water. They extend all the way south into the empty southwest corner of Texas, giving that state its most spectacular scenery in the Big Bend country. There the Rio Grande cuts a series of awesome canyons through the plateau between the Sierra del Consuelo and Sierra del Carmen on the Mexican side and the Chiso range in Texas. This strip of Texas is utterly uncharacteristic of the Lone Star State. The Franklin Mountains at El Paso, the Guadalupes, and the Chisos rival the most forbidding ridges of southern Arizona for rocky barrenness. It is a stony landscape of cactus, mesquite, creosote bush, and yucca.

The desert's invasion of New Mexico and Arizona is more successful. The Chihuahuan Desert flora spreads up the Rio Grande and other valleys for some 200 miles—almost as far north as Albuquerque—and the Sonoran Desert surrounds the timbered highlands of southern Arizona with its own distinctive species of cacti, grasses, shrubs, and thorn bushes. But deserts are a relatively minor feature of the Southwest's high west side. The story of both states is really the story of mountains, highland plateaus, and the sky.

The sky, the difference in the air, is partially responsible for the difference in the visual character of this high country. It's an effect that westbound air travelers can't fail to notice. Over Texas and Oklahoma the landscape below the airliner is, more often than not, at least partially obscured by clouds; even on clear days it is seen through layers of humidity, dim and hazy. As the plane crosses the prairie the haze thins and the land rises clear and distinct, like the shores of a distant continent emerging from the sea. This is partially due to diminishing moisture and partially to the effects of altitude. The earth's troposphere loses more than 3 percent of its density with each 900 feet of altitude. New Mexico and Arizona each average more than a mile above sea level, with their northern plateaus much higher. Thus when one looks from Flagstaff toward the San Francisco Peaks, or from Santa Fe

PUEBLO BONITO, CHACO CULTURE NATIONAL HISTORICAL PARK / NEW MEXICO

across the Rio Grande toward the glittering lights of Los Alamos in the Jemez Mountains, one looks through air that has lost a fourth of its weight. It is rich in hydrogen but thin in oxygen and carbon dioxide and thus offers less to refract and diffuse the light. The lights of Albuquerque, seen from Sandia Crest just above the city, lack the soft glow of the lights of Galveston and appear instead as a million glittering pinholes punched through the darkness. Eyes conditioned to the less transparent air of lower altitudes are deceived by distances—incredulous that the sharp blue outline on the horizon is a mountain range 100 miles away. And natives of this high, dry country find themselves suffering claustrophobic oppression under the heavy, hazy skies of Texas, Oklahoma, and points east.

The mountains affect the western skyscape, just as they affect everything in New Mexico and Arizona. They collect almost all of the area's scanty moisture. From early autumn through May, while the valleys are basking in sunshine, they accumulate layer after layer of snow—10 feet deep or more on the higher slopes—and become playgrounds for skiers and the source of water for irrigation. With spring runoff, it comes roaring down mountain streams into the Rio Grande, the Gila, the Salt, the Colorado, the San Juan, and the smaller streams. Once this meant devastating annual floods, but now reservoirs hold back the surplus, allowing extended irrigation seasons. In the summer, when the monsoon season brings moisture in from the Pacific, warm updrafts of air build towering cauliflower-shaped thunderheads over the mountain peaks, where they bombard the high country with lightning bolts before drifting away on the west wind. The last time I

was at Walpi on the rim of the Hopi Second Mesa in Arizona, I counted six such thunderstorms operating simultaneously. The largest had formed over Humphreys Peak and was obscuring the San Francisco Peaks with curtains of rain. Another was rumbling over the Black Mesa to the north, three smaller storms were drifting across the sky to the south, trailing narrow bands of water across the painted desert, and still another was forming far to the southwest over the Mogollon Rim. At Walpi the hot sun shone from a blue sky and, between the shadows of the thunderheads, the desert below was dappled with sunlight.

Unlike the Texas-Oklahoma end of the Southwest, where average rainfall lessens very gradually as you move west, differences in the mountain high country are abrupt and drastic, with altitude the determinant. Albuquerque, for ex-

PRICKLY PEAR CACTUS AND CASA GRANDE, BIG BEND
NATIONAL PARK / TEXAS

ample, receives eight inches of rain annually (enough for a rainy day in Houston). Sandia Crest, 10 miles from the city but about a mile higher, receives three times that amount. The west side of Santa Fe averages three inches less moisture per year than the northeast side— which has more than 1,000 feet greater altitude. Your street address determines whether or not you need snow tires.

This marked difference is visible no matter where you go in the two states. The short drive from the Tularosa Basin in southern New Mexico into the Sacramentos takes you from a landscape of cactus, creosote bush, and desert grasses into cool, spruce-fir forests carpeted with alpine flowers. Just north of Albuquerque the Simms ranch (not particularly large by New Mexico standards) included all but one of North America's biological life zones, from Upper Sonoran Desert to Hudsonian—a feat it accomplished by climbing from the Rio Grande to the top of Sandia Crest. In Arizona's equally vertical landscape more than 3,300 species of plants have been identified—believed to be America's broadest botanical spectrum.

As with Texas and Oklahoma, Arizona and New Mexico generally rise from south to north, but their mountain ridges and plateaus complicate the topography. In New Mexico, the Guadalupes, the Sacramentos, the San Andres, the Caballos, and the massive highlands of the Black Range extend southward almost to the Mexican border with fingers of desert landscape extending northward between them. New Mexico's most spectacular desert lies in the Tularosa Basin, the great rift between the Sacramentos and the Organ Mountain ridge. Within it are almost 200 miles of military bomb and missile ranges and an expanse of windblown ridges held in place by giant yucca, mesquite, and a great variety of prickly, almost leafless cacti. It also holds Lake Lucero, an ancient, dry lake bed that is now White Sands National Monument. It comes as near as anyplace on our continent to giving the appearance of total lifelessness. Across the flat floor of this ancient lake, 20 miles wide and 100 miles long, march mile after mile of great gypsum dunes, glittering white in the sunlight. They rise as high as 30 feet, moved inexorably northeastward by prevailing winds, their backsides firm, carved and sculptured by the moving air, their faces as soft as flour.

This high side of the Southwest is rich with such dramatic places, most of them seeming out of scale for human sight. In Arizona, there are the sculpture gardens of the Navajo National Monument, where immense fingers and thumbs of sandstone sprout from a floor of red sand; the wilderness of red, black, blue, and gray erosion of the cliffs of the Kaibab Plateau; and the endless carpet of green of the world's largest ponderosa pine forests spreading endlessly across the central highlands.

New Mexico has the aspen forests of the Sangre de Cristo Mountains—underfoot a yellow carpet of leaves, overhead a glittering blue-and-yellow ceiling of sky and leaves-not-yet-fallen, and floor and ceiling tied together with the stark black-and-white lines of ruler-straight aspen trunks. Bigger than life are the giant echo amphitheaters that seepage forms under the mass walls in northern New Mexico. There is New

LOG FRAGMENTS, BLUE MESA, PETRIFIED FOREST NATIONAL PARK / ARIZONA

Mexico's malpais, badlands of cooled lava spread below extinct volcanoes. Depending on its vintage, the malpais can resemble a lake of boiling, frothing black ink magnified to giant scale and somehow frozen mid-bubble. Or, when softened by eons of erosion, it can become a rolling, green-black plain, its basalt humps coated with multicolored lichens and its pits forming little rainwater pools lined with cattails and marshgrass. There is the saguaro cactus desert—fields of giant green exclamation marks, many sprouting thumbs, which defy simile because there is nothing else in nature like them. And there is the view from the Rio Grande Gorge bridge, where one can look down on the wings of golden eagles hunting rodents along the cliffs far below. The rapids of the river are 800 feet beneath your feet, a silver ribbon at the bottom of a great black lava slit. There is the monolith of Shiprock, the igneous core of a Pleistocene volcano, rising like a baroque cathedral with a thousand spires out of the rolling Navajo reservation grassland. There are the grotesque sandstone sculptures of the Bisti Badlands, which suggest the creations of a thousand Disneyland designers gone mad.

There are the Bosque del Apache marshes on a February morning when the sound carried on the cold dawn air is the conversation of a million birds—the odd fluting of sandhill cranes, the piping of red-winged blackbirds, the blended sounds of ducks, geese, grebes, herons, sandpipers, and scores of other species. And then, as dawn forms a hot pink glow behind the Sierra Oscura, the sudden roar of wings. Hundreds of snow geese rise from the marsh. Then thousands, rousing the Canada geese, and great flocks of greater sandhill cranes, and battalions of mallards, and pintails, and teal, until the sky is crowded. They rise above the bare cottonwoods, not like a rabble of blackbirds or crows, but in hundreds of separate, orderly formations. The air above is filled with the sound of geese. You see and hear what America was like when the Apaches used this lovely place as a camping ground.

The Apaches are gone from the Rio Grande now—the Mescaleros operating their ski resort on Sierra Blanca, the Jicarillas grazing their Herefords on New Mexico's edge of the Colorado Plateau, the Mimbrenos, the San Carlos, and the other bands keeping their culture alive in Arizona's White Mountain high country. But the Rio Grande, and the desert Southwest that lies west of it, is very much Indian country. Unlike my Indian friends in Oklahoma who had forsaken their old gods, the Navajos, Zunis, Hopis, Papagos, and the 17 little village-states where the Pueblo Indians live have kept their old religion and their old values alive and well.

Each morning when I drive to the University of New Mexico, and each evening when I go home, I see landmarks of this Native American Holy Land in which we live. Sandia Crest, looming over my rooftop at the east limits of the city, is Oko-Piu—the Turtle Mountain of Tiwa Indian mythology. This was the goal of the migration adventures of the Tiwas when they were new to this universe, the place Spider Grandmother taught them would be the center of their homeland. If you know where to look on the mountain you can visit the shrines where the kiva religious societies of the Rio Grande Pueblos leave their feathered prayer sticks as offerings, just as they were doing when the first Spanish explorers came up the river in the seventeenth century.

My favorite landmark (and my favorite mountain) is the one the white man calls Mount Taylor. As I drive west on Interstate 40 in the morning, the old volcano rises above the long, level line of Albuquerque's west mesa, snowcapped from autumn until spring, wearing a scarf of clouds on most summer days. It is 65 miles away, but it looks near enough to touch. Mount Taylor is Black Mountain for the Pueblo Indians, the place where the Twin War Gods dwell to warn their people away from the desert dangers beyond it. But for the Navajos (and for me) it is Turquoise Mountain, Tsoo'dzil, where the sky rests his left hand on Mother Earth.

West of the Rio Grande, the landscape is dotted with many such landmarks. San Antonio Mountain, the grassy old volcano cone north of Tres Piedras, New Mexico, was the place where Ute shamans communicated with God. Blue Lake, in the Sangre de Cristos above Taos, is the sacred home of the spirits that bless the people of Taos Pueblo. Black Mesa in Arizona is the home of the Navajo Black God and of the shrines of a dozen Hopi clans. Most sacred of all are the San Francisco Peaks, which rise above Flagstaff, Arizona. Humphreys Peak is the gateway between the worlds for the Hopis; for the Navajos, it is another of those mountains built by First Man, the place where the sky rests his forehead, and—like Mount Taylor—a place where the Navajo singers of curing ceremonials gather materials for their medicine bundles.

Once I climbed down into Canyon de Chelly, the deep sandstone slot cut into the Chuska Plateau northwest of Window Rock, Arizona, and spent a long summer day walking its sandy bottom, surrounded by its towering cliffs, engulfed in isolation. I found pictographs painted on the stone in sheltered places, most of them fairly modern Navajo stick-figure representations of Rainbow Man, Talking God, and other holy people. Not far from the so-called White House cliff ruins there was a faded image of the humpbacked figure of Water Sprinkler, a Pan-like deity of the Hopi Flute clan, who lived in this canyon before the Navajos came. The breeze had died and in the sudden silence I heard a whistle. It approached, a wavering, rising, falling sound like nothing I'd heard before. I found myself remembering that Water Sprinkler is usually depicted playing a flute. Then a dog trotted around the cliff, behind him a jostling column of goats, and behind the goats a Navajo boy. The goats were belled, and in this echo chamber below the cliffs their tinkling had been homogenized and merged into a single, singing sound.

I have other favorite places. The timeless stone adobe walls of Acoma Pueblo, the stone villages that perch on the Hopi Mesas, Zuni Pueblo on the night of the Shalako Ceremonial, the grandeur of Arizona's Oak Creek Canyon, the place in New Mexico's Jemez Mountains called Valle Grande, where a million years have converted a volcano caldera into a grassy bowl 14 miles long and rimmed with a collar of spruce and aspen. The list could be almost endless, but nothing on it could ever match the Grand Canyon.

It has been called the most spectacular sight on earth—this incredible, mind-boggling gap cut through the Kaibab

Plateau by the Colorado River. Erosion has been at work here for an estimated 65 million years, although geologists believe that much of the sculpturing we see today is the product of less than 10 million years. As seen from the rim, thousands of feet above its surface, the river is nothing but silver thread, implausibly small to have produced a chasm of such planet-splitting proportions, but that's only one of the optical problems the scene presents. A student of mine from Finland went to see it for a weekend and stayed more than a week. Why? "It was three days before my mind would accept it," she said. "It does not seem compatible with human reason."

The problem the mind has is variety as well as scale. At the rim, the first 100 yards of stone beneath your feet is Kaibab limestone, a tough, off-white rock, which fades into a layer of gray Toroweap formation of about the same depth.

Beneath this is Coconino sandstone, and next, a stripe of Hermit Shale about the color of dried blood. This rests atop 1,000 feet of mottled red-and-white Supai limestone. Each layer represents eons of the planet's formation. As you gaze at this stratification there is an awareness that you are looking backward through millions, perhaps billions, of years. The thick faded scarlet layer of Redwall limestone, which forms the stark cliffs below the Supai formation, was settled there when life on earth was new and limited to seawater. The pale tan stone on which it rests formed millions of years earlier, and the greenish Bright Angel shale was earlier still.

This green shale—tough and fine-grained—has resisted erosion better than most of the formations and forms the great flat table deep in the canyon known as the Tonto Rim. The lower canyon of the Colorado, the Inner Gorge, is cut

through this shale. Far below the Tonto Rim, the great river can be heard wearing away at the earth's bedrock, the Vishnu schist, which lies near the base of the earth's mantle and which formed more than a billion years before the planet knew life.

The Grand Canyon bedazzles its viewers with more than vastness, depth, or layering of colors. Each of its myriad strata seems to erode at a different rate and in a different way. Thus its walls are cut and carved into a hundred thousand forms. Each time the eye moves it focuses on something new and strange.

Among the dramatic surroundings of the Kaibab Plateau the flat world of the Panhandle hardly seems possible. And in the desert outside Yuma (where an old-timer once told me that "average annual rainfall is three inches, but it never

actually rains that much") the humid swamps of the Sabine seem memories of another planet.

Marie and I, who have spent our lives in both worlds of the Southwest, have learned to see these differences everywhere—from the way rainstorms form in the summer to the way such things as soda crackers and the human complexion become hard and dry in Arizona air and soft and moist in Texas. The seasons are different, and so are attitudes.

Why are attitudes different? Here's my theory: Most of Texas and Oklahoma seem designed for human comfort—fertile, well-watered, built to human scale, a land where living is easy. We see beauty here in fat cattle, lush cornfields, all those things that demonstrate that man has conquered the earth and made it flow with milk and honey.

In contrast, New Mexico and Arizona offer landscapes

Left– HAVASU FALLS, GRAND CANYON NATIONAL PARK / ARIZONA

Above– LOOKING WEST FROM TOROWEAP OVERLOOK, GRAND CANYON NATIONAL PARK / ARIZONA

that overpower man. He lives in oases where water supplies allow him to live. Thus much of the countryside is empty of human inhabitants. (I could walk 50 miles northwest from Albuquerque's west mesa with little risk of meeting anyone.) Mountains and deserts tend to keep man in perspective— aware that he is something small and impermanent on a very large planet. That affects attitude, and here's an illustration of what I mean:

A Navajo friend named Alex Atcitty was taking me to find a shaman who would tell me some things I needed to know about the Enemy Way ceremonial. Taking a shortcut across Rock Mesa on the way to Chinle, Arizona, Atcitty stopped his truck and pointed to the view. From the mesa rim we saw a 50-mile panorama of badlands drained by Bis E Ah Wash, a wilderness of stony erosion; flats of cracking white alkali deposits, gigantic humps of blue shale, cliffs of red clay, sandstone outcroppings carved by the wind and, here and there, great black intrusions of igneous rock. It is a landscape without water, poisoned by leached chemicals, without a blade of grass, without even the durable creosote bush or flatleaf cactus. It's as lifeless and inhospitable a place as you'll find this side of the moon. If Oklahoma had offered such a view we'd have named it the Pit of Desolation.

But Atcitty, a member of the Many Goats clan, was raised in the Chuska Mountains just east of here, and he was looking down at this desolation fondly.

"This is Hozhoni Teeh," Atcitty said.

That's Navajo for "Beautiful Valley."

I have now been away from the east end of the Southwest, and into the west end, long enough to adopt the Navajo attitude.

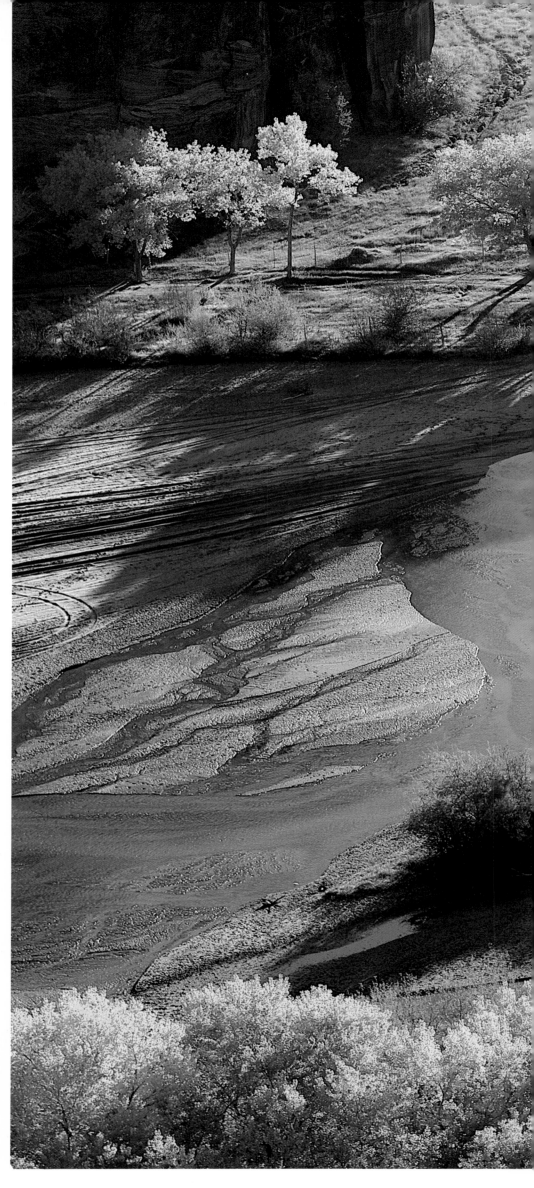

Left– SAGUARO CACTUS, PICACHO PEAK STATE PARK / ARIZONA

Above– AUTUMN, CANYON DE CHELLY NATIONAL MONUMENT / ARIZONA

Left– THUNDERSTORM, PANHANDLE COUNTRY / OKLAHOMA

Center– WICHITA MOUNTAINS NATIONAL WILDLIFE REFUGE / OKLAHOMA

Right– SHEEP'S HEAD, TRUCHAS PEAK, SANGRE DE CRISTO MOUNTAINS / NEW MEXICO

Left– YEI BE CHEI ROCKS, MONUMENT VALLEY NAVAJO TRIBAL PARK / ARIZONA-UTAH

Above– DUNES ABOVE SURF, PADRE ISLAND NATIONAL SEASHORE / TEXAS

SUNSET, TRINIDAD BAY / CALIFORNIA

Pacific America

Living Along the Ring of Fire

BY NEIL MORGAN

I LIVE ALONG THE RING OF FIRE. THIS IS THE folk name for that sensuous and unstable Pacific oval that follows the west coasts of both Americas, then loops across Alaska to Asia and meanders in a southerly direction about the western Pacific. In past eons, its turmoils thrust Hawaii up out of the Pacific. And today its earth faults set off tremors that titillate and terrify. Its volcanoes erupt and propel ash into the skies for thousands of miles, insuring extravagantly hued sunrises and sunsets for months.

All of this I know to be true, for I have seen and felt the furies of the Ring of Fire. But all I see of it from my study window is Devil's Slide, a benign ravine that leads from a residential street in California down to a Pacific surf where round boulders tumble over each other, their clatter reverberating across La Jolla Bay. The bay's surface is a calm and bewitching blue, a tranquil coverlet for a submarine canyon that no man has yet fathomed. We swim and sail over this canyon throughout our temperate seasons in Southern California, and seldom recall that if the Pacific Ocean were drained away, the gash in the earth's surface below us would appear

almost as sheer and deep as that of the Grand Canyon. Yet this is our swimming hole, and the Devil's Slide is an eroded coastal gully. Both are part of one of the most diverse shorelines in the world. Most Americans refer to it casually as the West Coast.

There are close to 5,000 miles of shoreline along our Pacific Coast from San Diego to the Strait of Georgia, where an invisible line in the water separates the United States from Canada. If one counts the shore of every inlet and bay and real and artificial island on this coast, California land meets water along a span of 3,427 miles. From north to south, if you glance across a map of America, you see that California stretches between latitudes comparable to those of Boston and Savannah along the Atlantic Coast.

Above California is the Northwest: Oregon and Washington, with shorelines so storm-battered and often gray that habitation moves inland for shelter, and only small towns of hardy fisherpeople and lumberers inhabit the coasts. Northwesterners' pride in their coastline approaches religious fervor. The people of Oregon exhibited this early: In 1913 they

Alaska
California
Hawaii
Oregon
Washington

reserved the state's shoreline for themselves, and even now they have unrestricted access to all but 23 miles of the bellicose sea along a 341-mile coastline. By contrast, almost two-thirds of the California coast is privately owned.

The Northwest coastline is a bonanza to the casual motorist. Driving between the Golden Gate at San Francisco and the Columbia River, which separates Oregon and Washington, you can see the shoreline in most areas without ever leaving your car. Since most of the Oregon coast is public land, it is a haven for those who hunt driftwood and the glass floats swept up by Pacific currents from the Orient, torn from fishing nets thousands of miles away.

The theme that pervades American history is westering. For many pioneers, the plains of the Heartland held dreams of land and freedom. Fur trappers pushed the frontier farther west, into the Rocky Mountains. But it was finally the land beyond the High Country that stirred passions and set off a massive, ongoing migration of Americans to the West Coast. First gold, then rich farmland, and soon more diverse visions

lured them. The name of California became magic, and within a century after gold was discovered at Sutter's Mill in 1848, the name had come to mean strange and marvelous things to the migrants, and to hundreds of millions who knew this distant coast only from rotogravures or from movie screens.

From the beginning and to each surprising new day, the allure of the Pacific Coast has been closely related to land, sea, and climate.

The wealth yielded in gold by California's Mother Lode was dwarfed by the fortunes of those whose farms fed the gold hunters. Vast valleys and hillsides of tall grass brought smart cattlemen west. With intricate irrigation on a scale unmatched since the Roman aqueduct, desert became farmland. Rivers were diverted. The indomitable Colorado River, drained and dammed and pumped over desert mountains, became the lifeline that transformed arid Southern California into tomorrowland.

Offshore fisheries from San Diego to Puget Sound lured migrants from the Old World: Portugal, Italy, Scandinavia. Verdant forests were cut to build cities and corporate em-

Overleaf–LA JOLLA COASTLINE / CALIFORNIA

pires, and yet enough trees still remain sheltered in state and national parks to provide wilderness sanctuary and an eternal magnet for tourists. The massive sequoia of the Sierra Nevada and the towering redwood of the foggy coastline are as exotic to most visitors as the palm trees of Hollywood. Striking, too, are those unlikely Southern California neighbors Mount Whitney, 14,495 feet high, and Death Valley, 282 feet below sea level, the highest and lowest points of the contiguous United States.

Even Hollywood owes it presence to sunshine and climate and the exotic locales that lured early moviemakers from studios in New York and Chicago to form the basis of an entertainment industry that shapes social mores and tastes around the world. It was the benign climate that brought the aircraft industry to the Pacific Coast. No single more specific example can be found than the move in 1934, by special trains, of a Buffalo, New York, company that was testing a new navy seaplane, and escaped Buffalo's ice for the open waters of San Diego Harbor to become the Convair division of General Dynamics.

While California grew to become the nation's most populous state, and Oregon and Washington swelled at a more sedate pace, enough wide-open spaces remained to hold appeal for the pioneers of the space age. It was to the dry lake beds of the high California desert that America's first space shuttle, *Columbia*, made its dramatic homecomings. There are still parts of California and the Northwest where you may drive for an hour or two without seeing a sign of human presence.

It is water, more than history or ethnology, that divides and causes friction between the people of Southern California and those in the north. In desert Southern California, about four of every five residents live within 40 miles of the sea; rainfall averages about 10 inches a year, almost all in winter. The north is rich in rainfall and free-flowing rivers. But the diversion of water by aqueduct and pipeline to the politically stronger south has polarized California. Range wars of bygone years pall beside the water wars of the more recent past, now most often fought out at election polls, in legislative halls, and in the courts. There are attorneys who have specialized solely in water rights along the Colorado River. Some judges have spent much of their careers hearing such lawyers invoke statutes unknown in other parts of the country.

Yet it is toward the shoreline and horizon that the people of the Pacific Coast face. This coast is the western climax of America; inland farming valleys and cattle ranges provide substance. Tall mountains and their parks—Yosemite is a star among them—provide sanctuary. Along the sea, currents that begin off Japan and New Zealand gnaw away at the jagged, outthrust arc of the Pacific Coast, throwing sand beachward in summer and eroding it with winter tides.

Probing the seas along this coast, early European mariners made their way warily northward; the first settlement was established above San Diego Harbor in 1769 after an overland trek by Spaniards from Mexico. More northerly seas forced back many explorers. Captains of Spanish galleons loaded with Philippine booty learned to follow trade winds across the Pacific to Cape Mendocino, at the apogee of Cali-

SEASTACKS, CANNON BEACH / OREGON

fornia's littoral, and then to coast south to Acapulco. Others' logs tell repeatedly of turning back southward in the face of heavy seas, fogs, and winds. But in 1792 Capt. Robert Gray, out of Boston, brought his brig *Columbia* in over a foaming bar and entered the glorious river he named the Columbia.

For decades thereafter, the land surrounding the river Gray discovered was known as the Oregon Country, and it was not annexed by the United States until 1846. Opposite the site that is now Portland, the Hudson's Bay Company set up its Oregon Country headquarters in 1824. Soon came Yankee fur traders, fish packers, farmers, and missionaries, moving northward into today's Washington. The transcontinental migrations of 1843 and 1845 were climactic for their era: They brought about 4,000 land-hungry settlers across the Oregon Trail.

From Devil's Slide outside my window I stare across the bay at sandstone cliffs which, in late light, take on the profiles of presidents. It is a foretaste of the long Pacific Coast shoreline: a high coastal littoral interrupted by wide beaches and valleys where dammed rivers once flowed. From San Diego northward to Los Angeles, the shoreline is built up almost solidly except for a 17-mile strip, part of Camp Pendleton Marine Corps Base. Newport Harbor, close by Disneyland in Orange County, is one of the great boating meccas of the southland, and then come the clutters of the industrial harbors of Long Beach and Los Angeles. Freeways and cities overwhelm this coast, and jets take off from Los Angeles International Airport over a denuded shoreline. Yet one evening not long ago a friend spoke wistfully of her childhood on a family ranch, part of an old Mexican land grant beside the sea. It took only a little probing to learn that it was Rancho Sausal Redondo, which became the city of Inglewood and Los Angeles Airport, itself a daytime community of more than 30,000. As the history of the land goes, such change in Southern California seems instantaneous.

Beside the urban sea of Los Angeles the dry and mostly barren Channel Islands begin to loom offshore. North of Santa Barbara the coast grows more pastoral. A long and lonely seafront has been sold in 100-acre parcels for gentleman farmers, with the seashore held in common. Nearby, one Sunday, in a century-old adobe house on another old ranch grant from the Mexican era, I visited Vicente Ortega, his white hair slicked back and his blue bandana knotted at his throat. He was lean and taut, but almost as old as the house. He had been a cowboy all his life here at the ranch called Arroyo Hondo.

"I used to come to this house to see my grandmother," he said. "I remember the Indian who helped my grandfather make this house. My aunt lived up the canyon near the pepper tree. That old olive tree up there, I had to water that when I was a kid. In those days there was land enough for everybody."

A few miles north, at Gaviota Pass, the coastal highway tunnels beneath cliffs that rise from the sea and eventually become the Tehachapi Range, transverse mountains that cross most of the state and mark the northern boundary of South-

Left– PROXY FALLS, CASCADE RANGE / OREGON

Right– SURGE AND FLOW, CARMEL COAST / CALIFORNIA

Below– SHROUDED GIANTS, SEQUOIA NATIONAL PARK / CALIFORNIA

Right– FAN PALM, NEAR SANTA BARBARA / CALIFORNIA

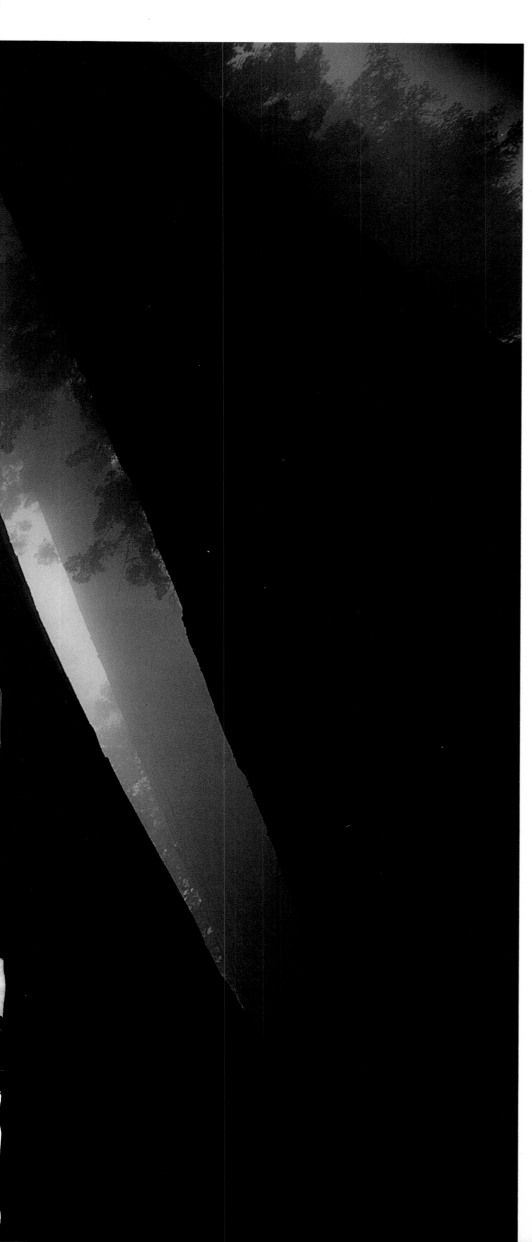

ern California. As one nears Point Conception, a central California landmark for sailors and seamen, the coast turns to run nearly due east and west. It becomes rolling range country, studded with live oaks, paralleling the inland Great Central Valley that is the agricultural heartland of California. Much of the destiny of this coast has been shaped in the valley, which extends more than 400 miles up and down the length of California, from 30 to 60 miles wide between coastal mountains and Sierra Nevada foothills. From Red Bluff at the north, the horizon southward is broken only once, by the Sutter Buttes, volcanic remains that rise 650 feet above flat, monotonous fields criss-crossed by irrigation canals.

About $14 billion in annual agricultural production comes from California, typically from 6,000-acre ranches hiring seasonal labor and using mechanical pickers. About one-third of America's canned and frozen vegetables and fruits come from this valley, including almost all of the commercial supply of pears, plums, prunes, grapes, and apricots. Most of the asparagus, broccoli, carrots, lettuce, and celery consumed in America is grown here. The bulk of the nation's figs, nectarines, olives, almonds, artichokes, dates, lemons, and walnuts come from here. The state ranks first in production of tomatoes, strawberries, beet sugar, beef cattle, turkeys, and second in cotton. Its wine industry is America's largest.

West of the coastal mountains, the monotony of the valley is contrasted by converging ocean tides that make central California waters nightmarish for small-craft sailors. At Big Sur, where the Santa Lucia range soars from the sea with ethereal abruptness, two-lane California Highway 1 winds 800 feet above the surf. The desert of Southern California is forgotten, and the coast becomes windblown and chilly. Cypress and pine cling in rocky crevices against the shear of wind along the Monterey Peninsula. It is 22 miles across

Monterey Bay, the setting of some of John Steinbeck's best writing. Past flat acres of artichoke fields, thriving in fog, one pushes northward toward Half Moon Bay. Soon the arches of the Golden Gate Bridge come into view.

To me there is no more stunning cleavage in nature than the Golden Gate of San Francisco Bay. Its visual drama is classic. Beyond that, it is the point of separation, geographically, botanically, and socially, between the California of legend, both past and present, and a pastoral northern coast that bears more kinship to the highland shores of Scotland and Wales. North from the Golden Gate the coast presents a thousand miles of rugged beauty along which one finds no cities. For almost 400 miles the largest town is Eureka, with about 30,000 people. The Pacific reaches full frenzy. At Duncan's Point, behind a barbed wire fence, a sign warns that 21 persons have been swept off the rocks to their deaths, each underestimating the reach of the waves breaking far below. (One learns to believe. To the north at Trinidad Head Light, Coast Guard annals report a wave in 1913 that "struck the bluff and shot over the level of the lantern." The light, then as now, is 196 feet above the sea.) But along Highway 1, the driver braves the headlands of the coast, crossing countless small streams and rivers jammed with splintered logs. After each, the highway climbs to a high meadow within sight of the sea. Weathered rail fences run beside the road, and firs and redwoods begin to appear. Lumber mills mix the scent of burning chips with smells of the sea. Among the ferns in spring the calla lily and iris thrive.

The San Andreas Fault, which slashes across California and which caused the San Francisco earthquake of 1906, can be traced easily by its seams and scarps as it moves over coastal mountains and then along the coast past Drake's Bay, where the British explorer Sir Francis Drake careened his *Golden Hind* in 1579, to brace it to carry on its load of silver booty from the Philippines. The San Andreas is a chilling reminder of the Ring of Fire. It passes hard by Fort Ross, where between 1812 and 1841 Russian sea otter hunters established the only Russian intrusion along this Pacific Coast. At Alder Creek, north of Point Arena, the fissure leaves the land and disappears in the floor of the Pacific. The seismic energy of the Ring of Fire, which geologists call the circum-Pacific seismic belt, is at its most visible in this vicinity. Point Reyes National Seashore moves northward about two inches a year while the mainland three miles across Tomales Bay is stationary. Some plant and animal species cannot endure even so slight a shift and are unable to survive on opposite sides of the bay. Lands on the west side of the San Andreas Fault strain to the northwest. In the past 15 million years, they have journeyed about 200 miles, in sudden and usually short, harmless wrenches.

The relatively gloomy countenance of much of the northern California and Northwest coastline carries with it the tensions of excitement and the enticement of danger. Some of the darkness comes from the lofty umbrellas of redwood trees. Majestic groves of them once graced slopes in a 20-mile-wide belt for more than 400 miles along the coasts of California and Oregon, reaching as far south as the Monterey Peninsula and Big Sur. Relatively few remain except in parklands, most of them concentrated in California's far northwest. Outside the parks one comes across lumber mills, fishing harbors, and steep coastal mountains. Wild rivers named Elk and Eel and Mad tumble down to the sea, leaving records of flood-level violence in their plains.

The world's tallest known tree is a 367-foot redwood near the harbor town of Eureka. Redwood National Park, of which it is a part, is a narrow preserve that is sometimes less than a mile wide and never more than seven miles from east to west. It straddles the coastal highway between Orick and Crescent City, halfway between San Francisco and Portland. The coastal redwood, *Sequoia sempervirens*, often grows from 200 feet to 300 feet in height. Its tapering trunk is bare of branches far above the ground; then its foliage explodes, feathery and delicate. It thrives in the coastal fogs so common to this region, in about 50,000 acres of state and national parks that span more than a 100-mile length of this coast.

Off to the west of the Humboldt redwood groves is a rugged promontory where, for more than 50 miles, there is no coastal highway; for decades it was referred to as California's Unknown Coast. In its midst the King Range rises a sheer 4,000 feet from the sea, a crossroads called Honeydew nestled in its lee. Nothing much is there but a country store and a tiny post office—and a rain gauge that has given Honeydew its sole distinction in the record books. One day Leonard Meland sat on the post office bench and told me of Honeydew's fame:

"For 29 years my wife Marie and I ran the store and post office. Part of my job was to measure the rainfall for the state of California. We had 178 inches one year. It never quit raining for 32 straight days. In one month alone in 1973 we had 46 inches. It can rain up to six inches a night."

Spreading his rain charts on his knee, he pointed up toward the wall of the King Range.

"Clouds come in off the Pacific and ride up and over the King like a roller coaster, and dump on Honeydew. That's how come we set rain records."

His little lesson is one that applies to much of Pacific America, where the weather comes from the ocean, borne inland by prevailing winds. Coastal mountains that extend along most of western America trap the moisture of the winds and dump it as rain at Honeydew, or as snow in the Sierra Nevada, or as the stuff of rain forests in the lee of the Olympic Mountain range in Washington's national parkland. This pattern also holds in Alaska, where high, steep snows are impacted to ice and begin their slow downward journey as glaciers. The same law prevails in the mountainous islands of Hawaii, where every visitor sees the contrasts of the lush windward sides of islands and the drier lee sides.

In the northwest corner of California, Crescent City is a town with an unlikely harbor. Its jetty is topped with 25-ton concrete tetrapods, like tumbled jacks. They were placed there soon after seismic sea waves, triggered by an earthquake at Anchorage, Alaska, a day earlier, flooded the town on March 28, 1964. (One of the heaviest of modern times, the earthquake destroyed parts of Anchorage; tsunami waves that followed it wiped out Valdez; the waves that struck little Crescent City moved with deadly aim, like rifle shots across

LIVE OAKS, SANTA YNEZ VALLEY / CALIFORNIA

the Pacific.) The fourth and worst of the waves that battered Crescent City during that night rolled over the town at a height of 21 feet and left 11 persons dead. The people of Crescent City can be forgiven for feeling put upon by nature: The waves traveled more than 1,700 miles from the Alaskan shore, and damage on the West Coast was confined to Crescent City.

Aboard a Coast Guard cutter one stormy December day I rode out of this harbor to the site of the worst maritime disaster in California history, the wreck of the side-wheel steamer *Brother Jonathan* in 1865. More than 200 people drowned when it grounded on St. George Reef, nine miles off Crescent City. Through dense fog around the reef I saw the looming bulk of a lighthouse like a gray castle. It was built in 1891; now, after claiming the lives of several of the Coast Guardsmen who manned it, it is automated.

Once the Oregon coastland was carpeted with forest almost 50 miles inland from the surfline. Douglas firs still persevere in awesome stands, their dark green fingering down into farmland and orchard. Oregon's Klamath Mountains follow an irregular angle to close off the top of the long parallel of California's coastal mountain ranges and the 450-mile Sierra Nevada, separated by the great trough of the agricultural Central Valley. As in California, quiet riches lie inland in the Northwest. Oregon breaks away from California along the 42nd parallel, where Spanish rule once gave way to British influence. Over the Oregon Trail came farmers and merchants who stood aloof from the California gold rush, and their towns and farms perpetuate the contrast. Many who settled Oregon came from New England, built church spires and trim white farmhouses, and gave settlements transplanted names like Portland, Salem, and Albany. Portland in Oregon and Seattle in Washington are the two large cities of the Northwest. Eastward across the wooded mountains from the sea rainfall diminishes, ranches swell in size, and sparseness rules. Eastern Oregon is one of the most rural sectors remaining in Pacific Coast states. Cattle graze in eastern Oregon and Washington, and wheat fields roll off to the horizon in postscript to the Midwest.

For a time the state of Washington seemed almost colonial, ruled from Seattle near the coast. Spokane has emerged as a strong farm center in the east, but rain is sparse at Spokane, and rain at Seattle is legend. Between Spokane and Seattle lies the Grand Coulee Dam, which gave birth to the aluminum industry of the Northwest in World War II and later facilitated the construction of the Atomic Energy Commission plutonium plant at Hanford.

Left– SAN JACINTO PEAK FROM SANTA ROSA MOUNTAINS / CALIFORNIA

Below– DUMONT DUNES, MOJAVE DESERT / CALIFORNIA

RAIN FOREST, ECOLA STATE PARK / OREGON

Up the center of Oregon and Washington marches the Cascade Range; rich valleys lie between it and the wind-blown coast. The best known of them is the broad Willamette Valley, the historic center of Oregon settlement and the site of Portland. Down to the coast through the Klamath Mountains flows the Rogue River, known and loved wherever steelhead and salmon fishermen are found. Coos Bay interrupts the sparseness of the southern Oregon coast to provide the world's largest lumber shipping port. Dunes soar to 200 feet halfway up the Oregon coast; state parks dot the shore, and sea lions lounge on offshore rocks. North of Tillamook, a coastal town famed for its cheese, is Seaside, where a monument marks the end of the trail for the Lewis and Clark Expedition of 1805, which had followed the mighty Columbia River to its mouth and opened it as a trade artery for the Pacific Northwest. The meandering delta of the Columbia is best seen from Astoria, where the 125-foot-tall Astor Column on Coxcomb Hill memorializes John Jacob Astor, who set up a fur trading station here in 1811.

Nowhere else along the Pacific Coast is there the insistent botanical lushness that is found along much of the Washington coast. From it one looks up to the distant Cascades, which separate the coastal area from the arid east. The tallest of the Cascades is Mount Rainier, 14,410 feet high. But the peak that most quickly reminds us of the Ring of Fire is Mount St. Helens, whose spectacular volcanic eruption on the morning of May 18, 1980, blew away almost a cubic mile of its summit and lowered its elevation from 9,677 feet to 8,364 feet. Continuing eruptions have left a familiar conundrum in this seismic ring: Will it continue to blow itself apart, or rebuild and surpass its former majesty?

Tucked cozily into the protected reaches of Puget Sound, Seattle is the center of Pacific America's forest and fishing industries. The Sound itself is a coastal marvel, part of a 200-mile extension of the Pacific that begins as the Strait of Juan de Fuca, along the Canadian border. This sea arm turns southward and becomes Puget Sound. Like Portland, Seattle is a seaport far from the sea. To its west, oceanward, rise the jagged peaks of one of the densest wildernesses on the American continent: the Olympic Peninsula, where rainfall reaches 135 inches a year. At the northern tip of the Olympic Peninsula one discovers a network of ferries that ply this island wonderland, some of them serving on Alaskan runs.

For many, the San Juan Islands are sacred in their beauty. There are 172 of them, lying between the United States and Canada's British Columbia in the southern end of Georgia Strait and the northern end of Puget Sound. Many of the islands are wooded and hilly. Their sandspits and glacial fjords are preserved by deed restrictions of private owners. Seaplane service is the only link with the outside for many of them. On some islands live families who find no reason to visit the mainland more than once every year or two. Others love these islands so much that they commute to their jobs in more urban areas, and their children use ferries to reach islands with schools.

When Alaska achieved statehood in 1959, the people of Seattle envisioned closer ties and economic boom; the Alaskan

gold rush, after all, had been a major factor in building Seattle as a city in the years after 1897. Alaska is more than eight times larger in area than the state of Washington. When it became the 49th state it increased the nation's area by nearly 20 percent. But much of Alaska remains unexplored—and unexploited—because of its difficult climate and terrain and its great distance from the rest of the States. Fewer than half a million people lived in Alaska at the time of the 1980 census, about 40 percent of them in or near Anchorage.

At the extreme northwest of the North American continent, Alaska embraces 586,400 square miles. It faces three seas: the Arctic on the north and northwest, the Bering on the west, and the Pacific on the south. The Ring of Fire slashes across Alaska's south face—one of the most active earthquake belts on earth.

Across the vast, ice-locked North Slope of Alaska, in the Land of Midnight Sun, Eskimos, Indians, and Aleuts share in the Native Claims Settlement Act of 1971, which placed 44 million acres and about $1 billion in trust for native-operated businesses. The North Slope oil field provided royalties that, among other things, erased Alaska's state income tax. About one-quarter of the state was set aside under the Alaska Lands Act in 1980, making a total of about 40 percent of Alaska conserved by state and federal agencies. The Lands Act tripled the United States' wilderness acreage, adding 56 million acres of Alaska land.

The popularity of pleasure cruising has brought many more visitors from the Lower 48 into Alaska's mainland Panhandle than into other areas of the state. The Panhandle includes a narrow, 400-mile-long archipelago that frames the Inside Passage, Alaska's heavily traveled Marine Highway, which snakes through narrow straits where mountain and forest close in from both sides. The closest habitation is sometimes 50 miles distant. Along its route are the capital city of Juneau, huddled like a giant's toe at the foot of precipitous 3,576-foot Mount Juneau; and the Mendenhall Glacier, an awesome prelude to the galaxy of 20 large glaciers within Glacier Bay National Monument. The bay itself is about 50 miles long, and the tongues of its glaciers reach out into the bay. A glacier named for the naturalist John Muir is among the most active. It is nearly two miles wide and has a face about 265 feet high. For those who visit Glacier Bay in summer, there is the memory of sound as well as sight: great hunks of bluish ice cracking off the glaciers and falling, with the reverberations of distant thunder, into the water.

Midway between Anchorage and Fairbanks, Mount McKinley, in Denali National Park, draws relatively heavy visitor traffic. At 20,320 feet, it is the highest peak in North America. Fewer Americans will see Gates of the Arctic National Park along the northern limit of wooded country. And it is a rare visitor who reaches Barrow, the northernmost of Alaska's towns, an Eskimo village with ice caves where Eskimo dances, carving, and blanket tossing are the major attractions. Barrow's brush with history occurred when Will Rogers and Wiley Post died in a plane crash nearby in 1935.

From Nome, an isolated town on Norton Sound in the far west, it is only about 120 miles across the Bering Strait to Siberia. No roads lead to Nome. Everything that does not

Above– CASCADE AT LOW WATER, ROGUE RIVER GORGE / OREGON

Right– PAINTED HILLS, JOHN DAY FOSSIL BEDS NATIONAL MONUMENT / OREGON

come by ship during the brief summer thaw must come by air. Fuel and supply ships unload a mile offshore and barge their cargo in; the sea is only three or four feet deep within a mile of Nome.

One day I flew north across the Arctic Circle from Nome to Kotzebue, an Eskimo town that extends like a fraying shoestring along a thin sandspit in Bering Strait. I wanted to see for myself this land that so few ever visit. Life here is harsh: In winter the trash is stacked out on the frozen sea, and in summer the permafrost melts just enough at the surface to make the land a quagmire. Along the beach in summer, wooden racks are laden with the black flesh of drying *oogruk* (seal) and strips of beluga (white) whale, which the Eskimos prize as food.

Yet not all is chill and harsh in Alaska. The permafrost-free, fertile soil of the Matanuska Valley, north of Anchorage, flourishes with grain, vegetable, and dairy farms, as does the farming area around Fairbanks, in the Tanana Valley. Here the land is still up for grabs. Homesteads of up to 160 acres can be acquired free from the U.S government, under certain conditions. The boom that accompanied the building of the Alaskan oil pipeline in the 1970s proved less than permanent, and vast areas of the state remain frontier.

Hawaii became the 50th of the United States within months after Alaska achieved statehood in 1959. Restless Americans who had westered across a continent now could leap by sea or air 2,397 miles beyond San Francisco and find themselves in a state capital. In land and climate, the two newest states dazzle by their contrasts. The stories of Jack London and the ballads of Robert Service tell of the bawdy Klondike gold diggers in Alaska; their tone is quite different from that of the enchanted Mark Twain, writing of what he called "the loveliest fleet of islands that lies anchored in any ocean."

The story of the creation of Hawaii brings us back to our Ring of Fire. The state is made up of the tops of submerged volcanic mountains; there are eight major islands. From west to east they are Niihau, Kauai, Oahu, Molokai, Lanai, Ka-hoolawe, Maui, and Hawaii. The volcanic eruptions that formed the islands have ceased on all but Hawaii, the easternmost and largest island. Volcanic activity is not uncommon on the highest Hawaiian mountains, Mauna Kea (13,796 feet above sea level) and Mauna Loa (13,680 feet). The repeated and dramatic eruptions of Kilauea in the winter of 1982-83 caused minimal damage but provided a veranda show for thousands of natives and visitors. It is the closest crater to Volcano House, a snug hostelry that draws thousands of thrillseekers. This island of Hawaii, known colloquially as the Big Island, is a wondrous volcanic triangle that soars out of the Pacific like an angry mastodon. Its old plantation towns, with their wood-frame churches, iron-roofed bungalows, and aging movie houses, seem to cry out of the 1930s. On the slopes of Mauna Kea, the venerable Parker Ranch claims

rank as the largest ranch under single ownership in the nation.

At Naalehu, the southernmost town of the United States, little meets the gaze but frame houses roofed in red iron, a schoolhouse in a playground that rambles to the edge of a sugar cane field, hedges of bougainvillea, a coffee shop and general store, small churches, and a monkey-pod tree that natives say was planted by Mark Twain. But there is a small road south from this southernmost town, and I turned down it one day with a native woman, Aala Akana. We drove through rolling grassland to Ka Lae (South Cape). Its ancient canoe moorings may mark the point where Maoris made first landfall after their heroic outrigger migrations, centuries ago, across 2,400 miles of sea from Tahiti. Shrines and temples of the ancient Hawaiians are being uncovered and restored near here. One built about 500 years ago by the Tahitian priest Paao has been stabilized as part of the Hawaii Volcanoes National Park.

The population of the state approaches one million, and almost seven of eight people live on the capital island of Oahu, where Honolulu and its fabled Waikiki Beach provide sybaritic symbols known around the world. Maui has become a bustling resort center, and so has Kauai, whose Na Pali Coast is one of the most idyllic in the world. It is an isolated 20-mile expanse of sheer drops, ribbon waterfalls, deep valleys, and overhanging cliffs. As with many of these islands' most stunning formations, the view of the land and sea from a helicopter is dazzling. A helicopter pilot once took me to the top of Kauai, not far from the Na Pali Coast. The restless white clouds that wrap mountain peaks here parted just long enough for us to swoop through, ducking around the edge of Waikoko Crater and landing atop 5,120-foot Mount Waialeale, the wettest spot on earth, getting an average of 472 inches of rain a year. Atop lonely Waialeale I saw a padlocked shack that housed the rain gauge. Nothing else. Lichens and stunted plants struggled in the volcanic soil against the wind and the deluge. The mountain is the source of all seven rivers of the island; they flow out to the sea like spokes of a wheel, forming the fertile valleys of the island where sugar cane, pineapple, and rice are grown.

We lifted off through the clouds and skimmed out over the same Pacific Ocean that I see from my study window in California at the foot of Devil's Slide. It surprises Americans of more traditional regions, but even across the great expanses of Pacific America, we feel a sense of neighborhood. Some think we live a bit dangerously along our Ring of Fire, but it is our own, and it is not dull.

STEPHEN HILSON / AlaskaPhoto

NANCY SIMMERMAN / AlaskaPhoto

NANCY SIMMERMAN / AlaskaPhoto

Left Top– SEASCAPE IN BEHM CANAL, NEAR
KETCHIKAN / ALASKA

Left Bottom– BLACK-LEGGED KITTIWAKES, NEAR
WHITTIER / ALASKA

Above– DISENCHANTMENT BAY AND HUBBARD
GLACIER / ALASKA

Above– HAENA POINT, NA PALI COAST, KAUAI / HAWAII

Right– CINDER CONES, HALEAKALA NATIONAL PARK / HAWAII